United States
Department of
Transportation

Volpe National
Transportation
Systems Center

July 2008

Auk Village Recreation Area

Conceptual Parking and Road Improvements Analysis

Report for U.S. Forest Service, Alaska Region, Tongass National Forest

TABLE OF CONTENTS

1 Introduction

The U.S. Forest Service, Alaska region, Tongass National Forest (USFS), plans to make improvements to the Auk Village Recreation Area (AVRA or recreation area) and specifically Point Louisa Road (the road or roadway) which passes through the AVRA. The USFS determined that these improvements are necessary to improve safety and facilitate management of the AVRA. The USFS asked the Volpe National Transportation Systems Center (Volpe) to review the latest USFS conceptual design, suggest modifications, and to develop additional conceptual designs.

The AVRA is a Forest Service day use facility located 15 miles northwest of downtown Juneau, Alaska, overlooking Auke Bay. It is a 67 acre, narrow and linear tract bordered on to the north by a drainage swale and steep densely wooded slopes, and to the south by steep slopes and Auke Beach. Vegetation on the south side varies from densely wooded to light brush. All recreation activity and facilities, except the Auk Nu Totem pole, occurs on the south side of the Point Louisa Road between the roadway and the beach. The only points of interest on the north side are the Auk Nu Totem pole and an interpretive sign with a small pull-off area.

Access to the beach is by steep stairways (7) and two ADA ramps from the roadway. At the foot of these steep slopes are open pavilions, covered picnic shelters, fire rings, picnic tables, paved walking paths, short trail bridges and lavatory structures.

The recreation area experiences heavy use. The intensity of this use varies throughout the year, and is weather dependent. In addition to the recreation uses, the road is used for access by residents east and west of the AVRA.

Currently there is little organization to parking and access. This lack of organization makes management of AVRA difficult and creates safety issues for pedestrians and traffic.

The USFS's design objectives are to:

- Enhance aesthetic values
- Provide a sense of arrival
- Improve parking capacity
- Provide traffic calming
- Improve pedestrian Safety

This report presents alternatives to the existing conceptual design and two additional concepts. The concepts discussed are:

- Two way traffic through traffic (existing concept)

- Cul-de-Sac option

- One way traffic

Variations with these concepts are discussed throughout this report.

2 Background

Point Louisa Road was previously part of Glacier Highway, the main roadway through the area. Alaska DOT completed construction of the Glacier Highway bypass in 2000 bypassing the AVRA and transferred control of the old portion of the Glacier Highway, Point Louisa Road to the USFS. The by-pass route roughly parallels the AVRA road for approximately a mile, offset by a distance of up to 0.25 miles upslope and separated by topography and tree screening.

Completion of the bypass created design opportunities for the AVRA. Several ideas had been discussed and some improvements have been completed. One opportunity is the

alignment of the roadway within the USFS land and parking improvements. The roadway is a paved two lane road with a posted speed of 30 mph, though actual speeds are higher. The only parking for visitors to the AVRA is along the southern shoulder off the road. These parking areas are unmarked, and as a result parking is disorganized and haphazard (see photo). There is no separation of parking and pedestrians from  through traffic. During peak periods, cars park close to the roadway.

Historically, this area was heavily used by the Auk tribe, and continues to be an important cultural site. Much of the area between the road and beach is likely source of archeological artifacts of the Auk Tlinglit people. Any design proposals should be sensitive to these areas.

The trees on the slopes between the roadway and the Glacier Highway Bypass to the north provide a buffer for the AVRA. This area is sensitive because these trees are exposed to winds off Auk Bay and are subject to windthrow. Disturbance to this area such as felling trees or grading changes alters the forest edge and increases the windthrow risk to the remaining trees. Maintenance of this buffer is important to the character and attraction of the AVRA.

3 Methodology

In preparing this report, Volpe Center engineer:

- Reviewed the latest conceptual design and accompanying narrative
- Visited the site and met with a USFS civil engineer
- Revisited the site to observe existing conditions, take photographs and observe traffic and visitor activity
- Developed three alternatives based on an analysis of site conditions, constraints, and objectives
- Composed a brief description of each alternative
- Participated in a teleconference to discuss the alternatives
- Finalized the alternatives based on comments collected during teleconference
- Prepared this report.

The conceptual design goals were to meet the design objectives and minimize disturbance to the sensitive areas with the AVRA. These designs meet the USFS's design objectives within the smallest practical footprint.

4 Existing Conditions

The existing roadway is benched into hillside. The roadway is confined between the wooded area to the north and the Auke Bay area to the south. This confinement creates the major challenge to meeting the USFS's design objectives.

5 Conceptual Design Alternatives

The Volpe Center team developed three principal design concepts for the AVRA roadway to meet the above design objectives while minimizing the impacts to the trees to the north and sensitive areas to the south. The included conceptual designs represent the smallest practical footprint that meets the design objectives within the design constraints. Additional elements such as center islands, chicanes, and roundabouts would increase the project footprint and disturbance to the site. Based on our analysis of the site, we believe that these elements are not necessary because the required safety improvements can be achieved through less intrusive means—namely, by relocating parking spaces adjacent to the activity areas to the south (thus minimizing pedestrian-vehicle conflicts), by segregating parking from through traffic, and through visual narrowing of the roadway using 11-foot lanes, shoulder surface treatments, and wayside barriers such as post and chain to reduce vehicle speeds.

The Volpe Center team developed three design concepts for the AVRA roadway to meet the Forest Service's design objectives.

5.1 Design constraints
- Maintain trees and other vegetation between the AVRA and the Glacier Highway Bypass north of the project. Minimize potential windthrow to the remaining trees.

- Minimize disturbance to the slope south of the project to protect Auk Village cultural sites and potential culturally sensitive areas.

- Ensure 20 feet of curb-to-curb distance for access by fire department vehicles

The narrow linear nature of the site creates a conflict between these constraints.

5.2 Design objective solutions

Provide a sense of arrival

The existing Welcome sign at the eastern end of the AVRA indicates entrance and arrival for through traffic and visitors. The segregated parking proposed in the three concepts presents additional opportunities to create a sense of arrival for visitors. Opportunities include welcome signs or information boards as visitors enter the parking areas.

Enhance aesthetic values

All three concepts create visual order by segregating visitor activities and parking from through traffic. They also eliminate the negative visual effects of the disorganized, informal parking.

Improve parking capacity

Information provided by the USFS indicated the current "legal" parking capacity is about 80 vehicles, though actual counts can be higher on busy days when parking spills into unauthorized areas. These proposed designs provide approximately 150 spaces including accessible spaces, 3 RV spaces, and one tour bus space.

Provide traffic calming

The width of the roadway and distinguishable treatment of the shoulders will visually create a feeling of narrowness that is associated with reductions in vehicle speeds. Speed bumps located in the parking aisles provide more deliberate calming where the most visitor activity occurs.

<u>Improve pedestrian safety</u>

The proposed parking layout segregates all visitors from through traffic. Visitors can unload their vehicles and move back and forth to the recreation area without being exposed to traffic in the through-lanes. A raised crosswalk would provide access to the totem pole area on the north side of the road.

5.3 Design standards

- Parking space dimensions: 60 degree angled parking, 10' wide x 19.5' deep
- Parking Aisle: 15' wide unless otherwise noted
- Design Vehicles: See vehicle templates in Section 9
- Roadway Cross section as below

Pavement width for the oneway option is 20' with an 18' travel way.

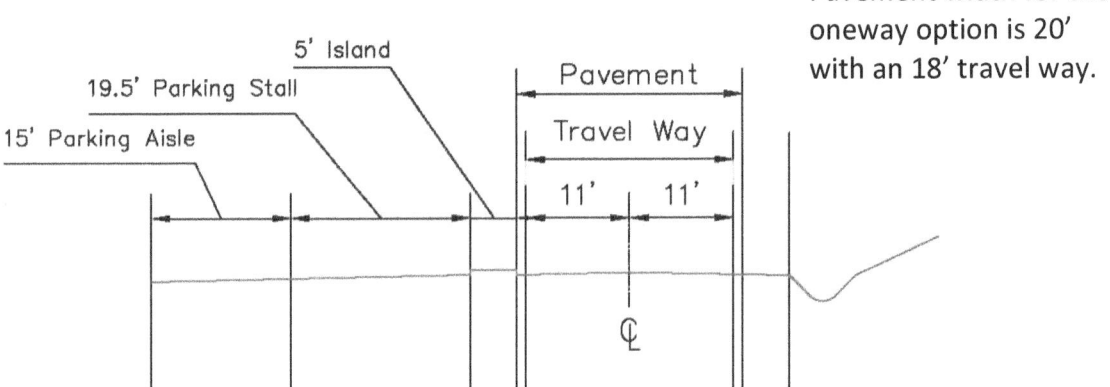

TWO WAY TRAFFIC ROADWAY CROSS SECTION
N.T.S.

5.4 Elements common to all options

The parking trays for all options are single loaded (parking on one side of the aisle only). The Volpe Center team selected angled parking and a 15' aisle width to minimize the width required along the entire project and the disruption to the areas north and south of the road. The trade-off is that this maximizes the length of disturbance. The USFS may instead consider using double loaded trays near areas that are less sensitive. This approach would encroach further over the southern slope, but allow more sensitive areas to remain undisturbed while maintaining the same number of parking spaces.

- Parking for all passenger cars, pickup trucks and other light vehicles is completely segregated from through traffic and located on the south (beach) side of the road.
- A contiguous walkway traverses the entire site connecting all principal beach areas. A delineated cross walk provides access to the Auk Nu Totem Pole. This is the only access to the north side of the roadway.
- Improved pedestrian safety by isolating parking from through traffic.
- Three RV parking spaces and one 40' tour bus space are provided. Spaces are pull-in/pull-out spaces that eliminate the need for these larger vehicles to back up. The exact location of the tour bus space can be adjusted; in the diagrams, it is shown near the pavilion or near the roundabout depending on the alternative.
- Intrusion of the project area beyond the top of the south slope is minimized but not eliminated. This represents a carefully considered trade-off between pedestrian/vehicle safety and site disruption.
- Traffic flow/parking: Because most visitors to AVRA arrive from the east end of the road, the three concepts allow westbound drivers to check the availability of spaces before entering a parking area. This scheme requires these drivers to make a left turn to enter the parking areas. This is discussed in more detail for each option.

5.5 Option 1: Two-Way Traffic with modifications to most recent conceptual design

Option 1 is the modification to the existing USFS conceptual design concept. It maintains two-way traffic and allows access/egress from the west and east ends of AVRA.

Features include:

- Two 11' wide travel lanes and two 1 foot paved shoulders. Total pavement width is 24 feet. Islands between traveled way and parking are 5 feet wide.
- Width of construction: 63.5 feet plus 5' sidewalk. The sidewalk may be separated from the roadway where practical to increase pedestrian segregation and minimize disturbance to sensitive areas.

This scenario avoids sending all exiting traffic through the western residential area. Most visitor traffic would enter and leave the area at the same point at the eastern end of the site.

If the Forest Service determines that the left turns create a conflict with eastbound traffic, they could prohibit left turns into the parking areas and require all westbound traffic to use the roundabout to reverse direction. Under this scenario, the parking angle could also be reversed to maintain arriving motorists' ability to allow all drivers to check the availability of spaces before entering a parking area.

5.6 Option 2: No Through Traffic: Terminate the west end of the road near camping area

Option 2 is similar to Option 1 except that the road ends at the west end and the roundabout becomes a cul-de-sac.

Option 2 features include:

- Two 11' wide travel lanes and two 1 foot paved shoulders. Total pavement width is 24 feet wide. Islands between traveled way and parking are 5 feet wide.
- Width of construction: 63.5 feet plus 5' sidewalk.

This option avoids sending any traffic through western residential area. All traffic enters and leaves the area through the east end of the AVRA. This reduces potential left turn conflicts because access from the west is eliminated. If the USFS finds that left turn conflicts still exist, the same options described for Option 1 would apply to this option.

Although this option prohibits normal traffic through the west end, final design should provide for emergency through access at the west end. The USFS could install a break a way gate, an unlocked turnstile, a locked gate with a Knox-Box®, or other similar access controls to control access through the cul-de-sac.

5.7 Option 3: One-Way Traffic from east to west

This Option makes the road one way from east the west. Option 2 features include:

- One 18' wide travel lane and two 1 foot paved shoulders. Total pavement width is 20 feet wide. Islands between traveled way and parking are 7 feet wide.
- Width of construction: 61.5 feet plus 5' sidewalk.

This option directs all exiting traffic through west residential area. Visitors from the west residential area must backtrack on the Glacier Highway bypass to enter the area. The USFS has the option to allow access to the camp grounds from the west under this layout. This option eliminates left turn conflicts into parking areas.

The major downside to this option is poor circulation within AVRA. If optimistic visitors are unsuccessful when searching for a parking space close to their destination, they would have to drive through the residential area and backtrack on the bypass.

6 Management considerations

Segregated parking common to all options allows the USFS to control vehicle access to the recreation area's facilities with minimal to no impact to the roadway. Control may minimal using only signs or more direct with gates. Certain parking areas could be closed off at certain times in accordance with USFS management priorities.

Option 1 and to a lesser degree Option 3 maintain through traffic flow for non-visitors. Option 2, the dead end option, provides almost exclusive use to AVRA visitors. The more exclusive the roadway is to AVRA visitors, the more the USFS would be perceived to be the responsible party for maintenance and traffic enforcement; e.g., the City and Bureau of Juneau may be less inclined to plow this area in winter. The USFS may consider this an advantage or disadvantage.

7 Other design considerations

7.1 Stormwater management and erosion control

There is a drainage swale along the north side of the roadway. Several culverts collect runoff from the swale and discharge on the slope along the south side of the roadway. The discharge from these culverts causes erosion of the slope and some rutting at the beach.

All options will disturb the existing drainage swale. The final design should utilize similar natural swales wherever possible instead of pipe. This will improve infiltration and detention. Collecting runoff in pipes eliminates infiltration and detention and concentrates discharge at a few points along the beach.

The rutted areas at the existing discharge points should be engineered and maintained with rip-rap and filter fabric to control erosion.

8 Summary

The table below summarizes the major distinctions between the three options.

SUMMARY OF EFFECTS		
Option	Advantages	Comments
1 Two way – Through Traffic with modifications to existing design	Minimal change to existing traffic patterns Avoid sending additional traffic trough west residential area	Potential issue with left hand turns. USFS could consider prohibiting left hand turns
2 Dead end – Cul-de-Sac	Reduces non-visitor traffic through the area	USFS should provide emergency access at roundabout
3 One way through traffic	Minimizes turning conflicts	All traffic must exit through the west residential area Poor/limited circulation within the AVRA

9 Design Templates

The turning used for these conceptual designs are from AASHTO, *Geometric Design of Highways and Streets*, the "Green Book."

NOTE: Intercity bus template was used to check turning radii for Tour Bus.

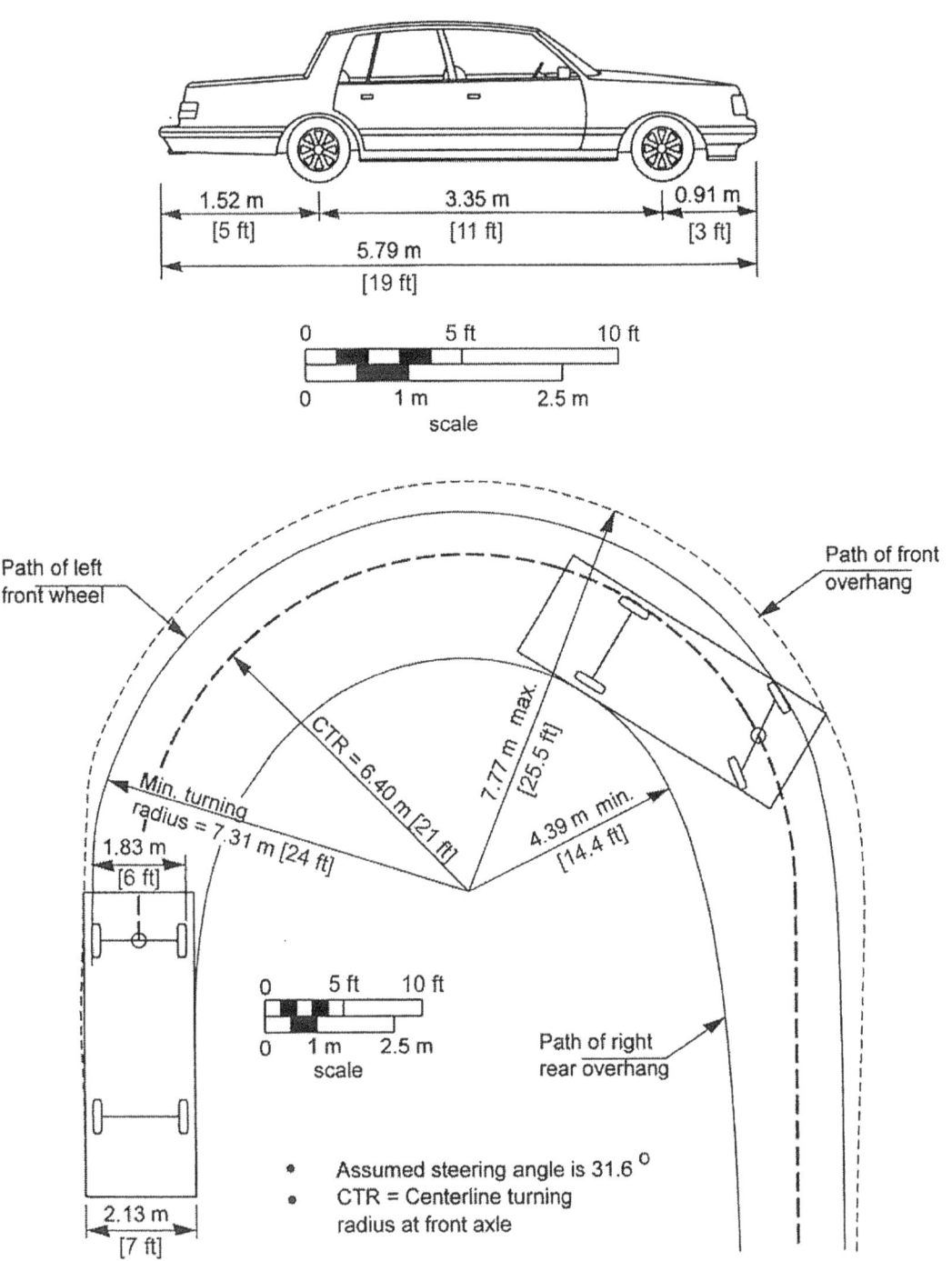

1.52 m
[5 ft]

3.35 m
[11 ft]

0.91 m
[3 ft]

5.79 m
[19 ft]

0   5 ft   10 ft

0   1 m   2.5 m
scale

Path of left
front wheel

Path of front
overhang

CTR = 6.40 m [21 ft]

7.77 m max.
[25.5 ft]

Min. turning
radius = 7.31 m [24 ft]

4.39 m min.
[14.4 ft]

1.83 m
[6 ft]

0   5 ft   10 ft

0   1 m   2.5 m
scale

Path of right
rear overhang

2.13 m
[7 ft]

- Assumed steering angle is 31.6°
- CTR = Centerline turning
  radius at front axle

Exhibit 2-3. Minimum Turning Path for Passenger Car (P) Design Vehicle

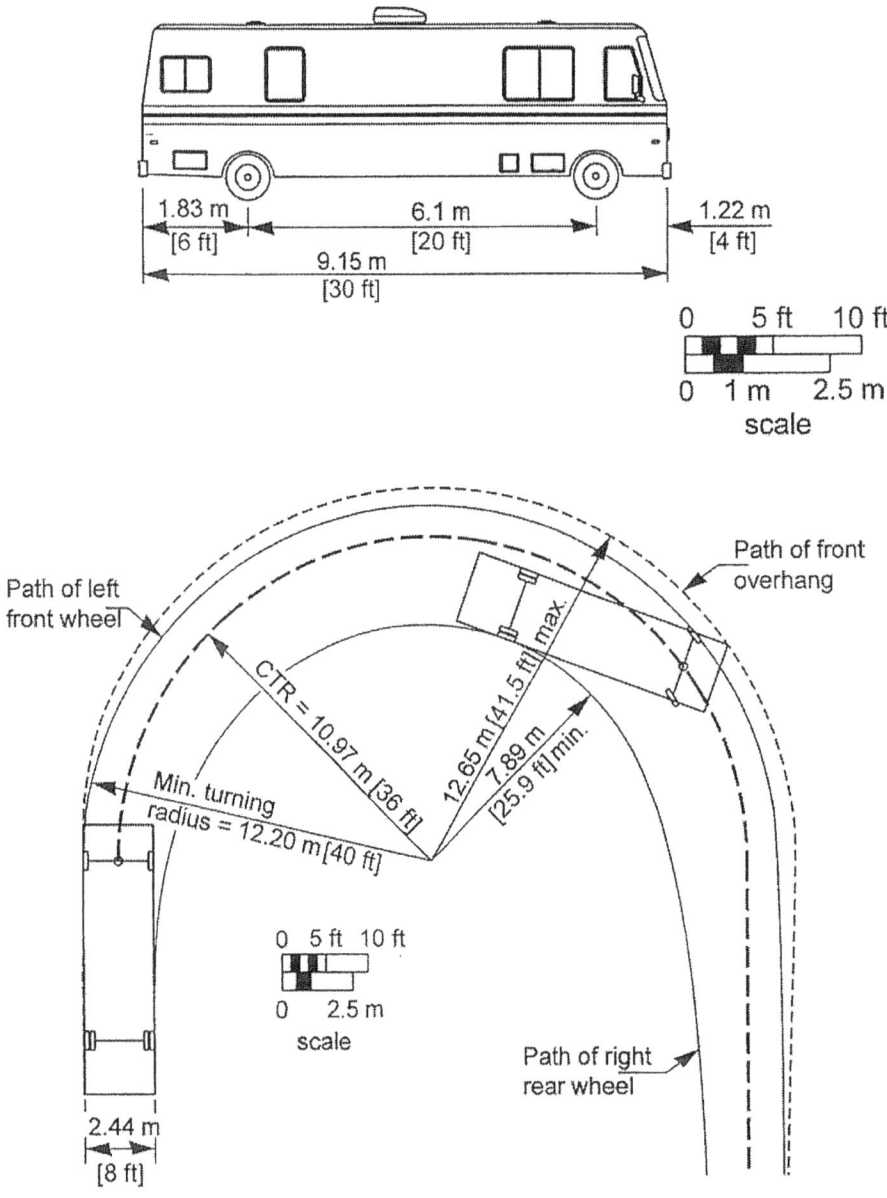

- Assumed steering angle is 33.7°
- CTR = Centerline turning radius at front axle

Exhibit 2-20. Minimum Turning Path for Motor Home (MH) Design Vehicle

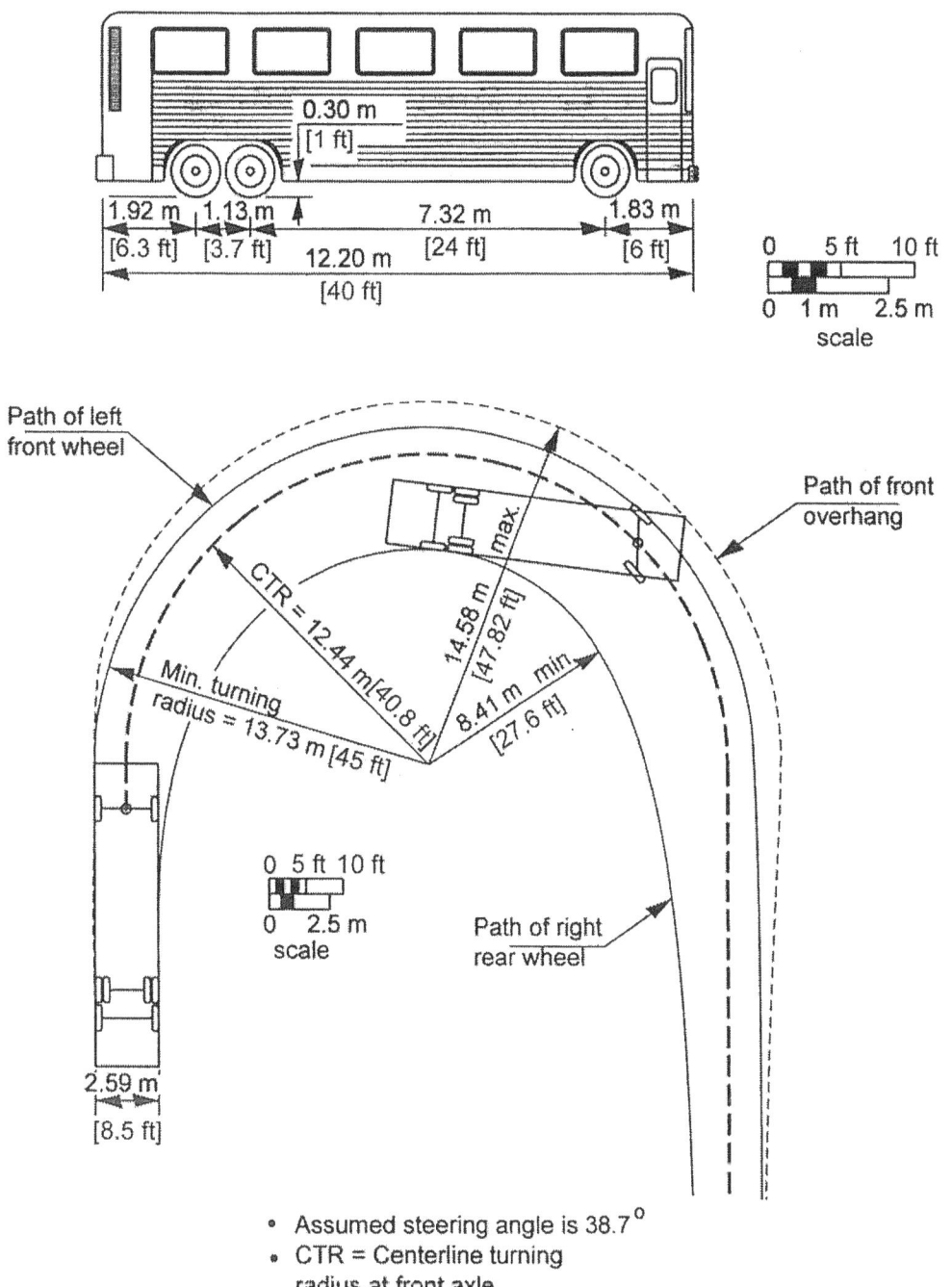

- Assumed steering angle is 38.7°
- CTR = Centerline turning radius at front axle

Exhibit 2-5. Minimum Turning Path for Intercity Bus (BUS-12 [BUS-40]) Design Vehicle

10 Drawings

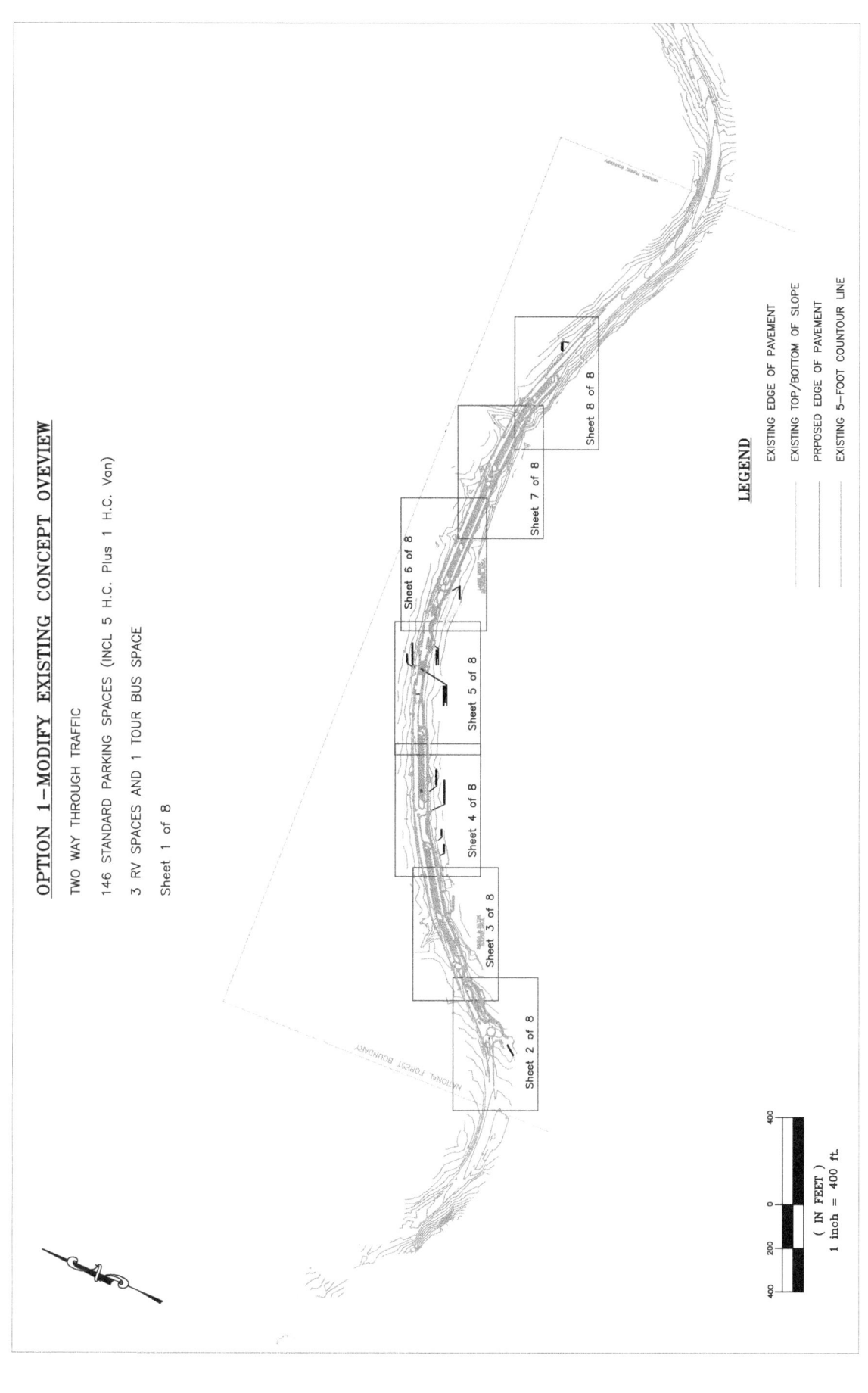

OPTION 1—MODIFY EXISTING CONCEPT OVEVIEW

TWO WAY THROUGH TRAFFIC

146 STANDARD PARKING SPACES (INCL 5 H.C. Plus 1 H.C. Van)

3 RV SPACES AND 1 TOUR BUS SPACE

Sheet 1 of 8

Sheet 2 of 8

Sheet 3 of 8

Sheet 4 of 8

Sheet 5 of 8

Sheet 6 of 8

Sheet 7 of 8

Sheet 8 of 8

NATIONAL FOREST BOUNDARY

LEGEND

EXISTING EDGE OF PAVEMENT

EXISTING TOP/BOTTOM OF SLOPE

PRPOSED EDGE OF PAVEMENT

EXISTING 5-FOOT COUNTOUR LINE

400   200   0   400

(IN FEET)

1 inch = 400 ft.

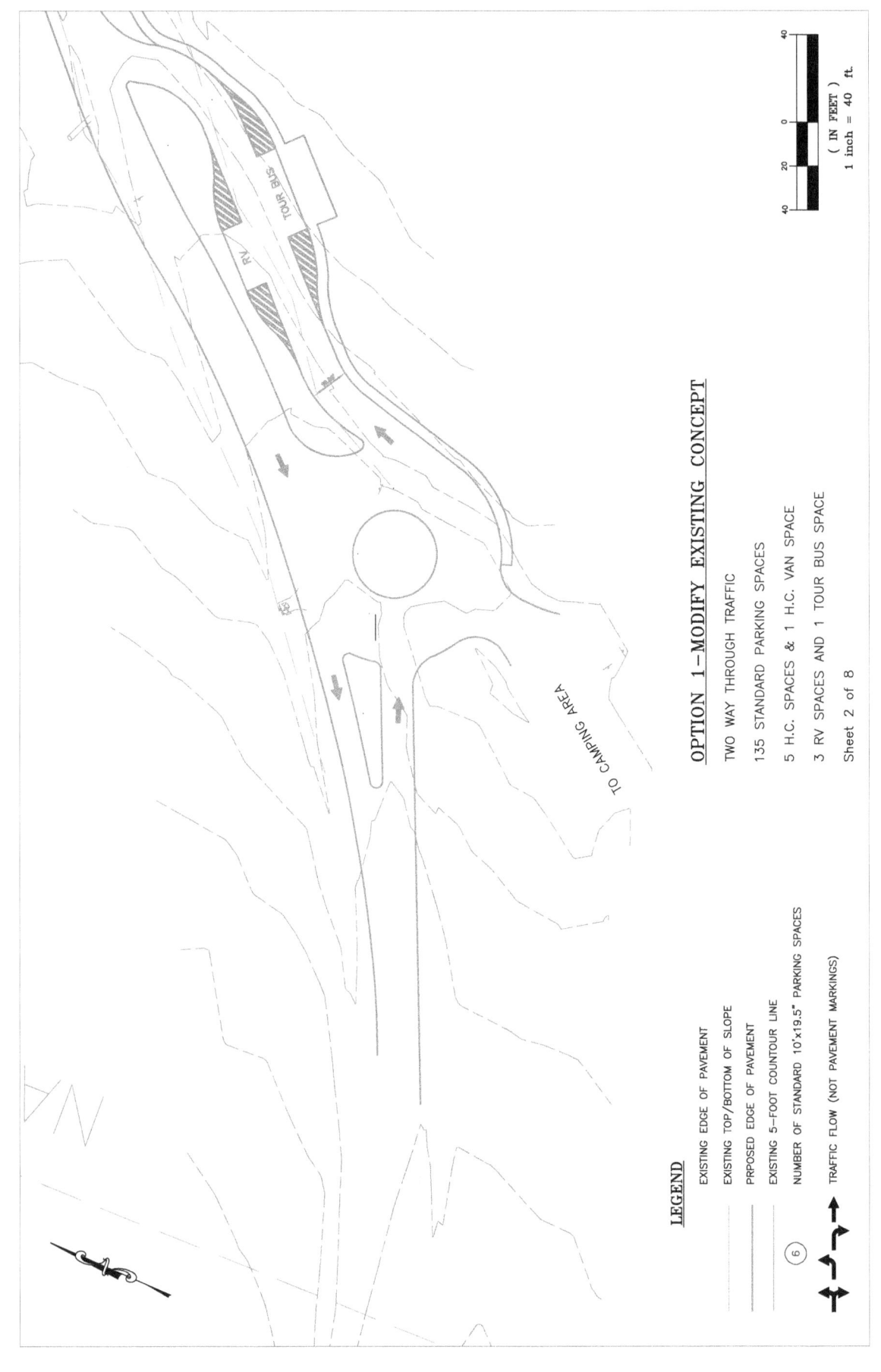

RV

TOUR BUS

TO CAMPING AREA

OPTION 1-MODIFY EXISTING CONCEPT

TWO WAY THROUGH TRAFFIC

135 STANDARD PARKING SPACES

5 H.C. SPACES & 1 H.C. VAN SPACE

3 RV SPACES AND 1 TOUR BUS SPACE

Sheet 2 of 8

(IN FEET)
1 inch = 40 ft.

<u>LEGEND</u>

EXISTING EDGE OF PAVEMENT

EXISTING TOP/BOTTOM OF SLOPE

PRPOSED EDGE OF PAVEMENT

EXISTING 5-FOOT COUNTOUR LINE

NUMBER OF STANDARD 10'x19.5" PARKING SPACES

TRAFFIC FLOW (NOT PAVEMENT MARKINGS)

6

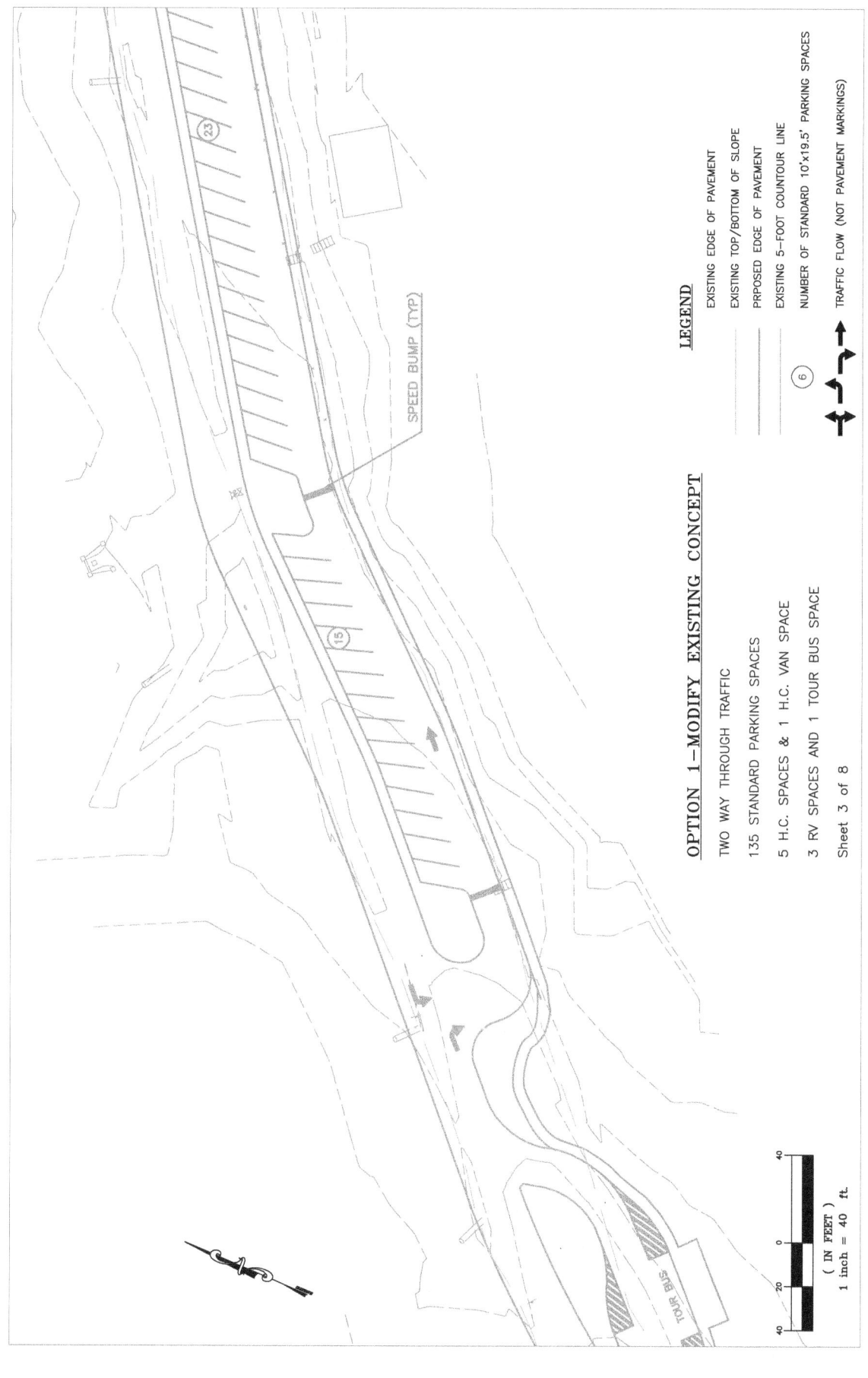

OPTION 1—MODIFY EXISTING CONCEPT

TWO WAY THROUGH TRAFFIC

135 STANDARD PARKING SPACES

5 H.C. SPACES & 1 H.C. VAN SPACE

3 RV SPACES AND 1 TOUR BUS SPACE

Sheet 3 of 8

LEGEND

EXISTING EDGE OF PAVEMENT

EXISTING TOP/BOTTOM OF SLOPE

PRPOSED EDGE OF PAVEMENT

EXISTING 5-FOOT COUNTOUR LINE

⑥ NUMBER OF STANDARD 10'x19.5' PARKING SPACES

TRAFFIC FLOW (NOT PAVEMENT MARKINGS)

SPEED BUMP (TYP)

TOUR BUS

(IN FEET)
1 inch = 40 ft.

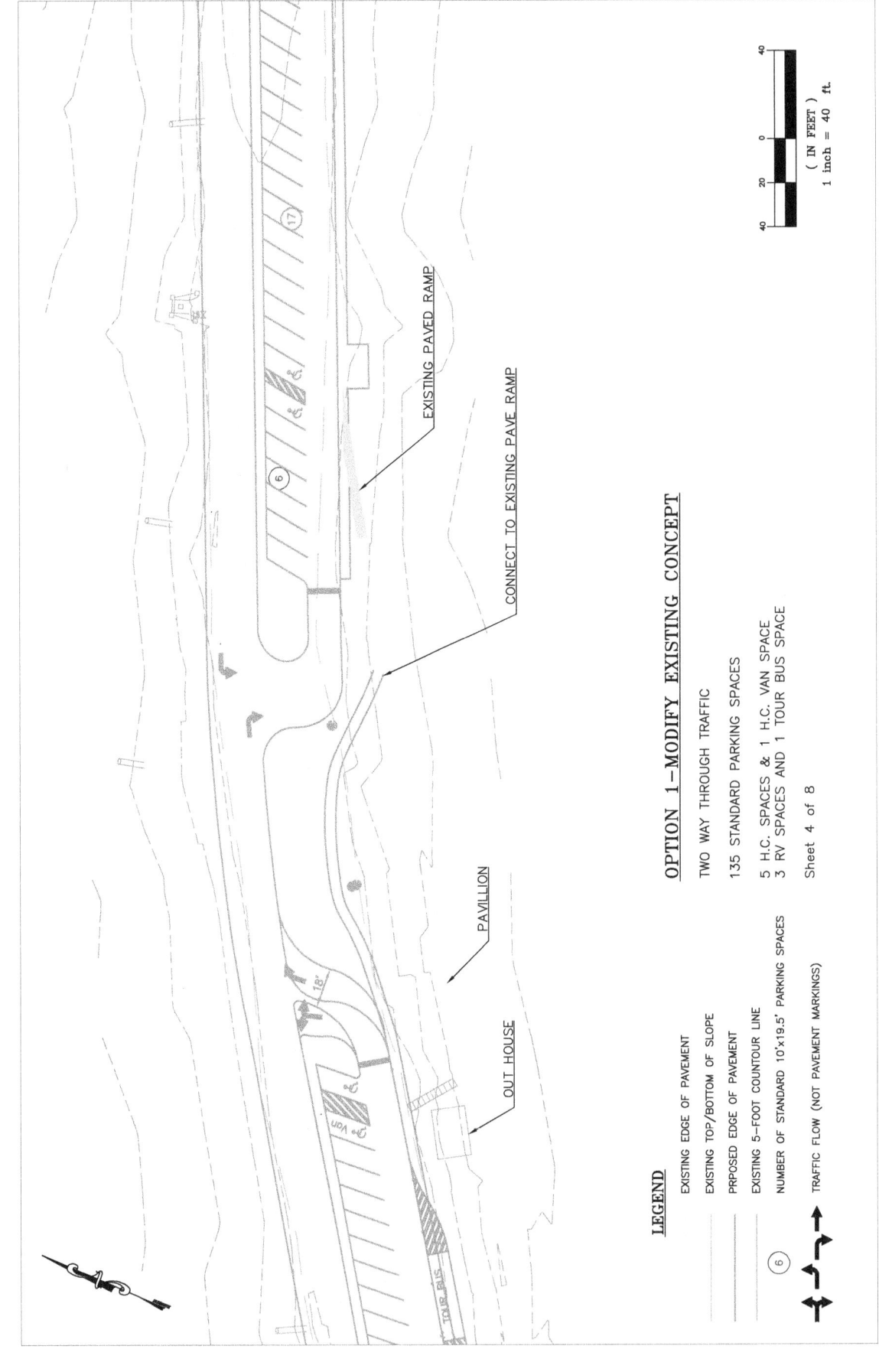

EXISTING PAVED RAMP

CONNECT TO EXISTING PAVE RAMP

PAVILLION

OUT HOUSE

18'

TOUR BUS

OPTION 1-MODIFY EXISTING CONCEPT

TWO WAY THROUGH TRAFFIC

135 STANDARD PARKING SPACES

5 H.C. SPACES & 1 H.C. VAN SPACE
3 RV SPACES AND 1 TOUR BUS SPACE

Sheet 4 of 8

LEGEND

EXISTING EDGE OF PAVEMENT

EXISTING TOP/BOTTOM OF SLOPE

PRPOSED EDGE OF PAVEMENT

EXISTING 5-FOOT COUNTOUR LINE

NUMBER OF STANDARD 10'x19.5' PARKING SPACES

TRAFFIC FLOW (NOT PAVEMENT MARKINGS)

(IN FEET)
1 inch = 40   ft.

40   20   0   40

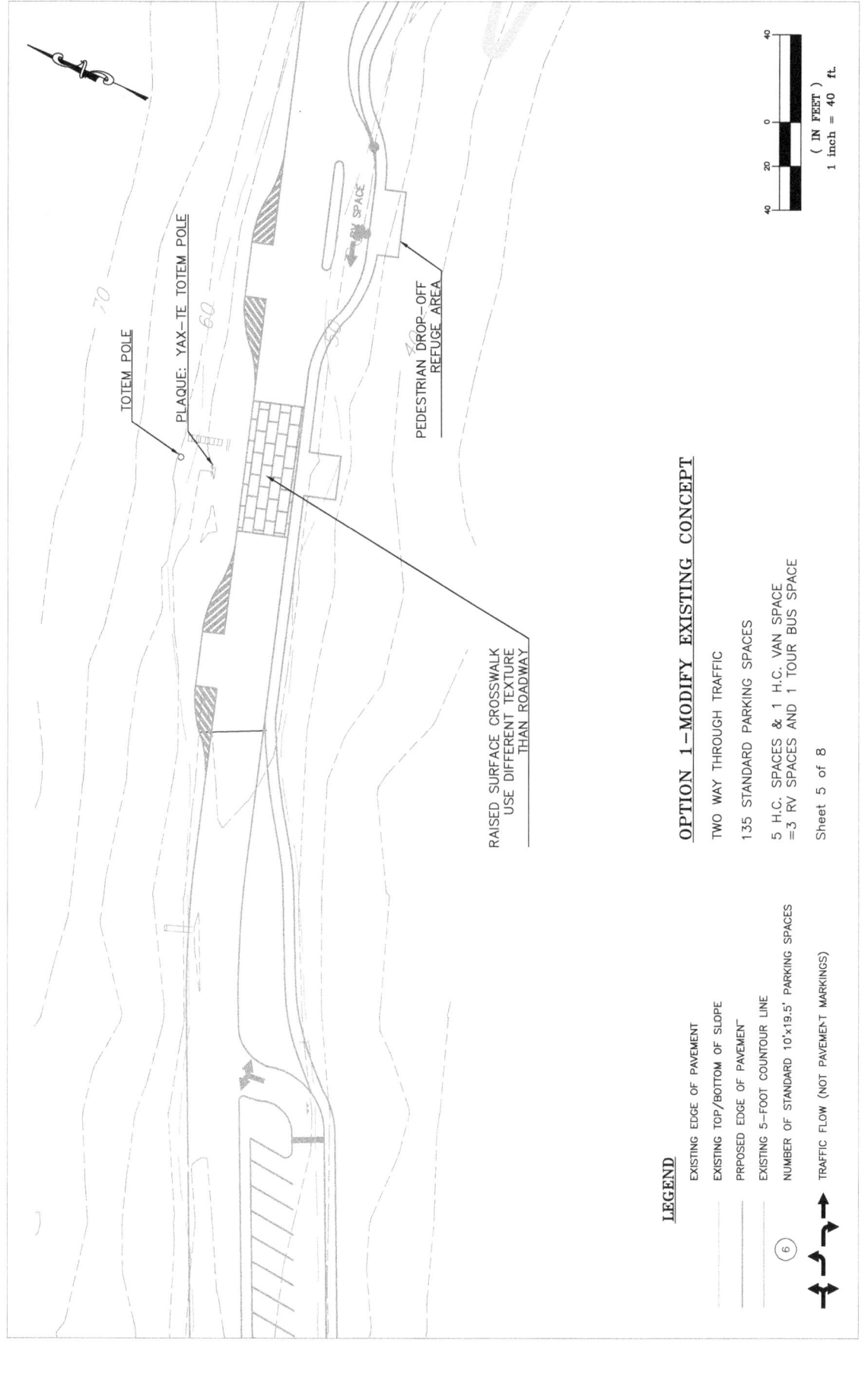

TOTEM POLE

PLAQUE: YAX-TE TOTEM POLE

RAISED SURFACE CROSSWALK
USE DIFFERENT TEXTURE
THAN ROADWAY

PEDESTRIAN DROP-OFF
REFUGE AREA

SPACE

70

60

40

OPTION 1-MODIFY EXISTING CONCEPT

TWO WAY THROUGH TRAFFIC

135 STANDARD PARKING SPACES

5 H.C. SPACES & 1 H.C. VAN SPACE
=3 RV SPACES AND 1 TOUR BUS SPACE

Sheet 5 of 8

LEGEND

EXISTING EDGE OF PAVEMENT

EXISTING TOP/BOTTOM OF SLOPE

PRPOSED EDGE OF PAVEMEN'

EXISTING 5-FOOT COUNTOUR LINE

NUMBER OF STANDARD 10'x19.5' PARKING SPACES

(6)

TRAFFIC FLOW (NOT PAVEMENT MARKINGS)

(IN FEET)
1 inch = 40 ft.

40   20   0   40

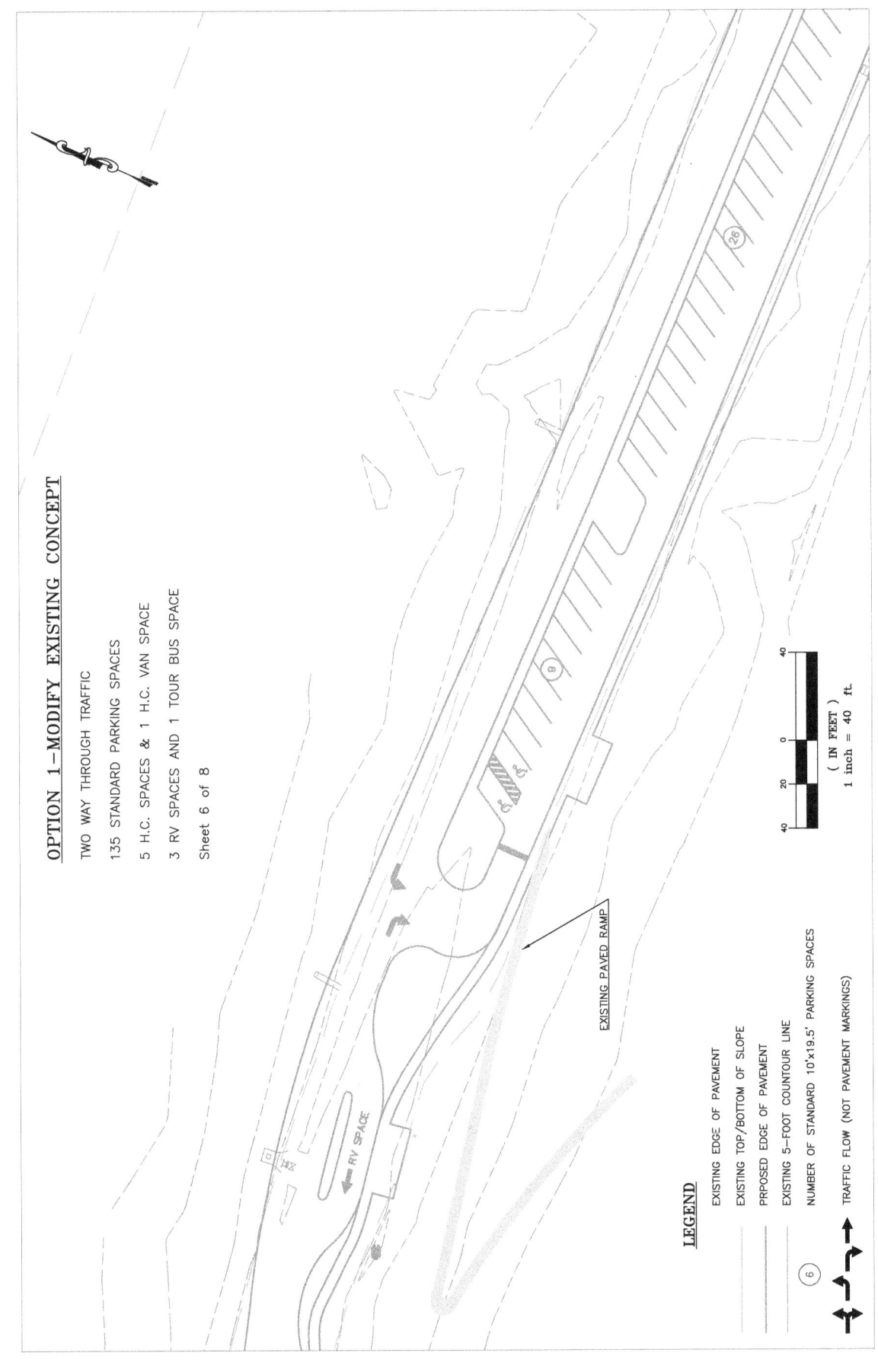

OPTION 1—MODIFY EXISTING CONCEPT

TWO WAY THROUGH TRAFFIC

135 STANDARD PARKING SPACES

5 H.C. SPACES & 1 H.C. VAN SPACE

3 RV SPACES AND 1 TOUR BUS SPACE

Sheet 6 of 8

RV SPACE

EXISTING PAVED RAMP

(IN FEET)
1 inch = 40 ft.

LEGEND

EXISTING EDGE OF PAVEMENT

EXISTING TOP/BOTTOM OF SLOPE

PRPOSED EDGE OF PAVEMENT

EXISTING 5-FOOT COUNTOUR LINE

NUMBER OF STANDARD 10'x19.5' PARKING SPACES

TRAFFIC FLOW (NOT PAVEMENT MARKINGS)

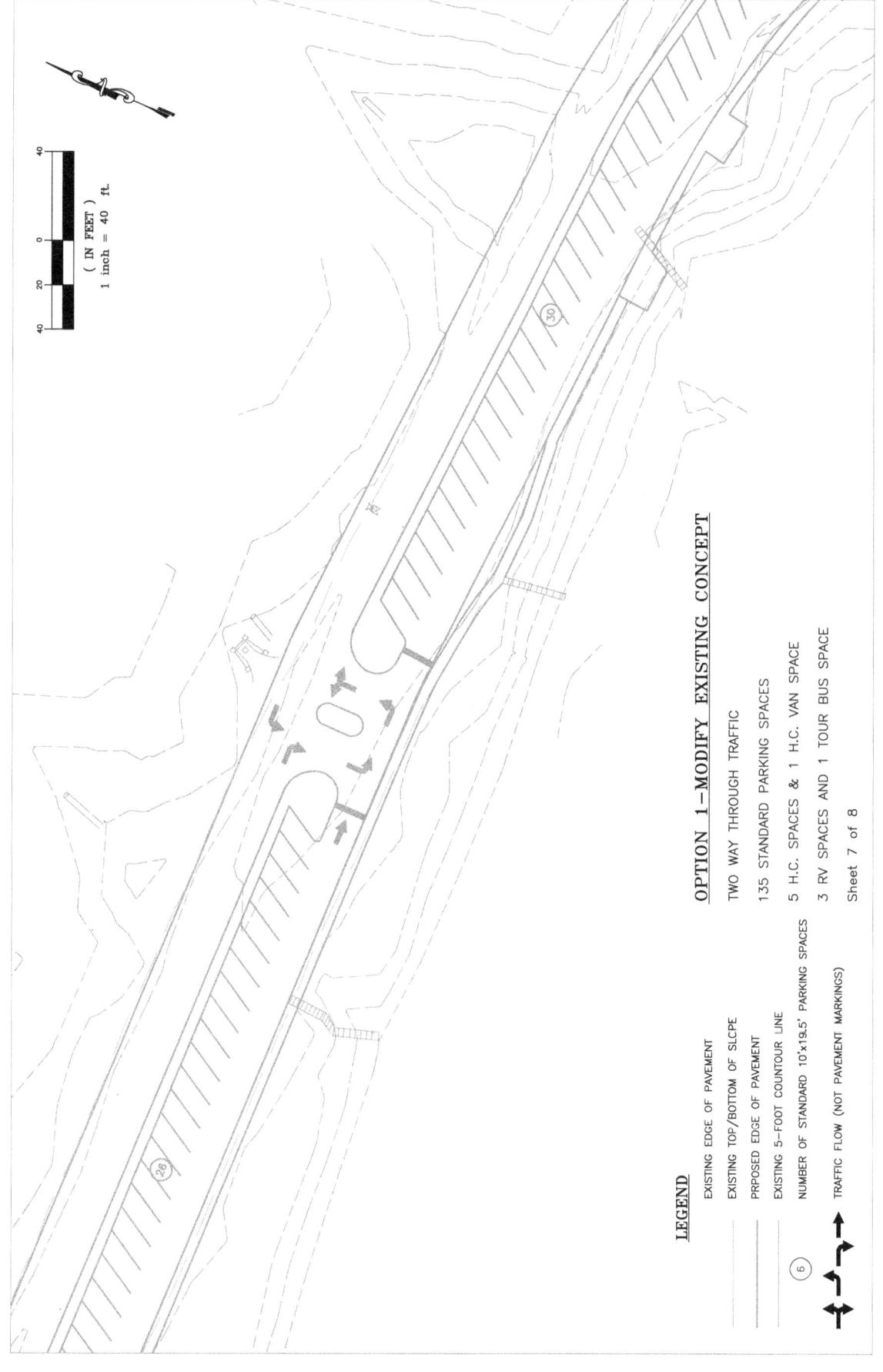

LEGEND

EXISTING EDGE OF PAVEMENT

EXISTING TOP/BOTTOM OF SLCPE

PRPOSED EDGE OF PAVEMENT

EXISTING 5-FOOT COUNTOUR LINE

NUMBER OF STANDARD 10'x19.5' PARKING SPACES

TRAFFIC FLOW (NOT PAVEMENT MARKINGS)

(IN FEET)
1 inch = 40 ft.

OPTION 1—MODIFY EXISTING CONCEPT

TWO WAY THROUGH TRAFFIC

135 STANDARD PARKING SPACES

5 H.C. SPACES & 1 H.C. VAN SPACE

3 RV SPACES AND 1 TOUR BUS SPACE

Sheet 7 of 8

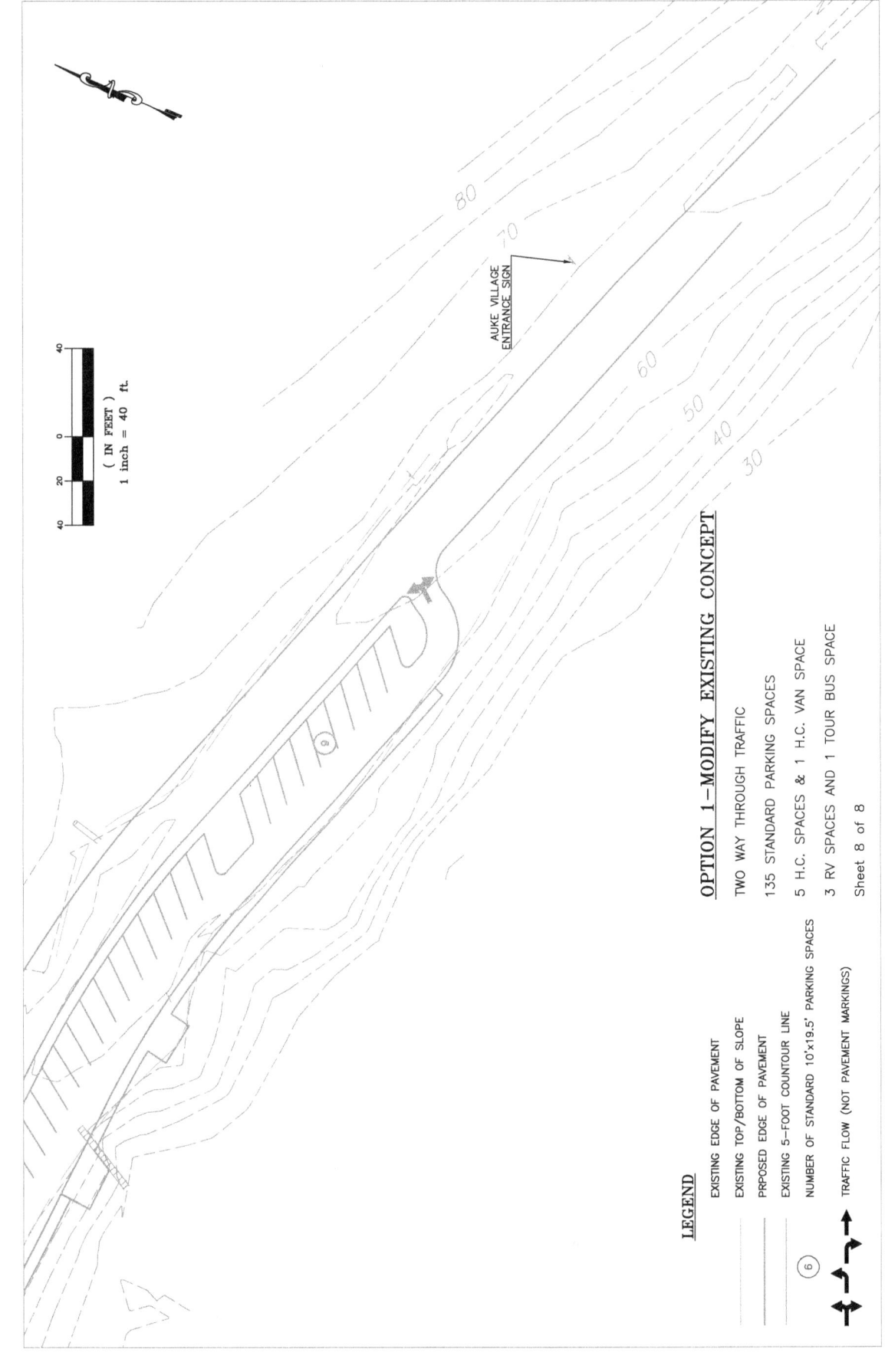

(IN FEET)
1 inch = 40 ft.

AUKE VILLAGE
ENTRANCE SIGN

LEGEND

EXISTING EDGE OF PAVEMENT

EXISTING TOP/BOTTOM OF SLOPE

PRPOSED EDGE OF PAVEMENT

EXISTING 5-FOOT COUNTOUR LINE

NUMBER OF STANDARD 10'x19.5' PARKING SPACES

TRAFFIC FLOW (NOT PAVEMENT MARKINGS)

OPTION 1—MODIFY EXISTING CONCEPT

TWO WAY THROUGH TRAFFIC

135 STANDARD PARKING SPACES

5 H.C. SPACES & 1 H.C. VAN SPACE

3 RV SPACES AND 1 TOUR BUS SPACE

Sheet 8 of 8

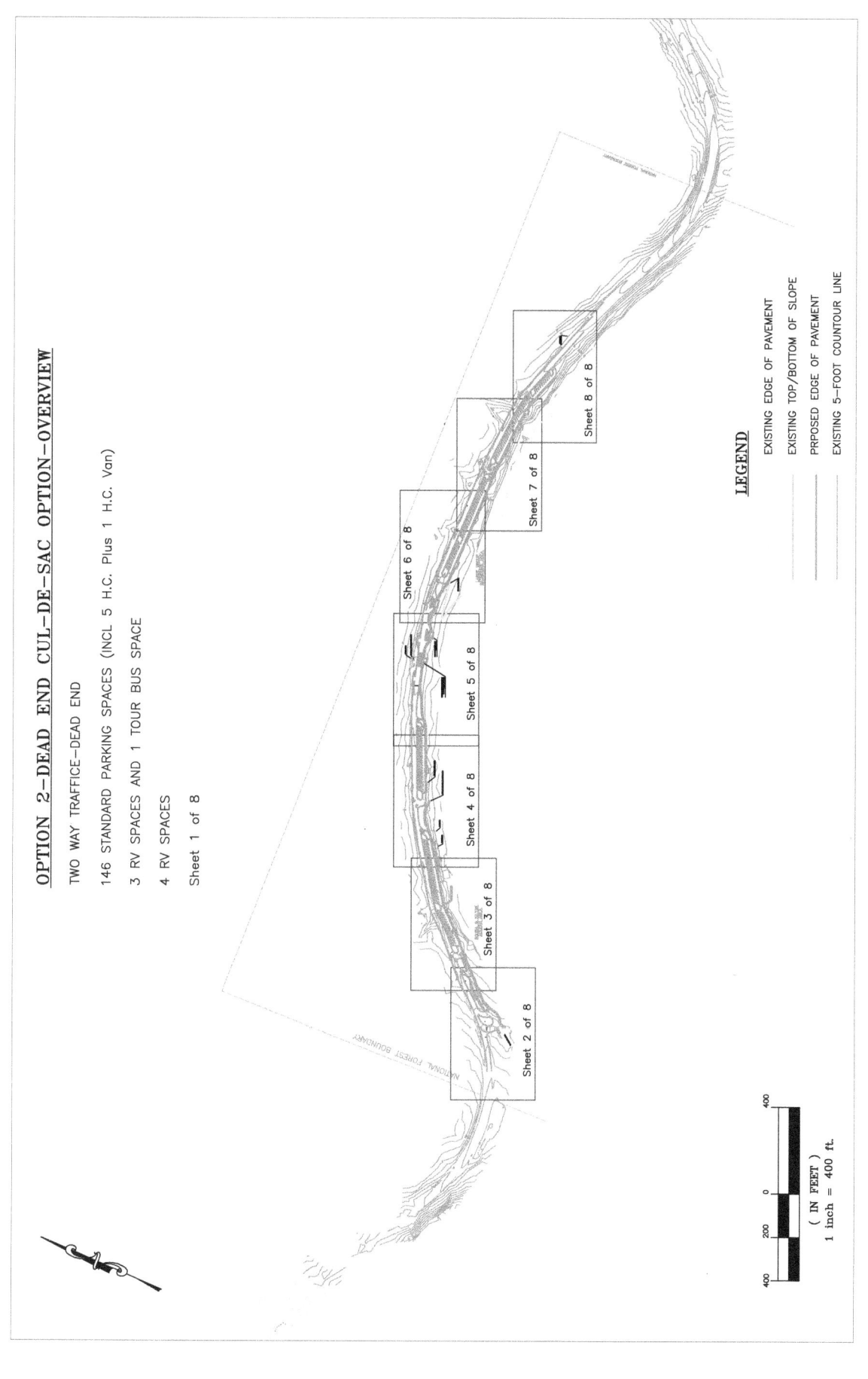

OPTION 2-DEAD END CUL-DE-SAC OPTION-OVERVIEW

TWO WAY TRAFFICE-DEAD END

146 STANDARD PARKING SPACES (INCL 5 H.C. Plus 1 H.C. Van)

3 RV SPACES AND 1 TOUR BUS SPACE

4 RV SPACES

Sheet 1 of 8

Sheet 2 of 8

Sheet 3 of 8

Sheet 4 of 8

Sheet 5 of 8

Sheet 6 of 8

Sheet 7 of 8

Sheet 8 of 8

NATIONAL FOREST BOUNDARY

LEGEND

EXISTING EDGE OF PAVEMENT

EXISTING TOP/BOTTOM OF SLOPE

PRPOSED EDGE OF PAVEMENT

EXISTING 5-FOOT COUNTOUR LINE

400   200   0   400

(IN FEET)
1 inch = 400 ft.

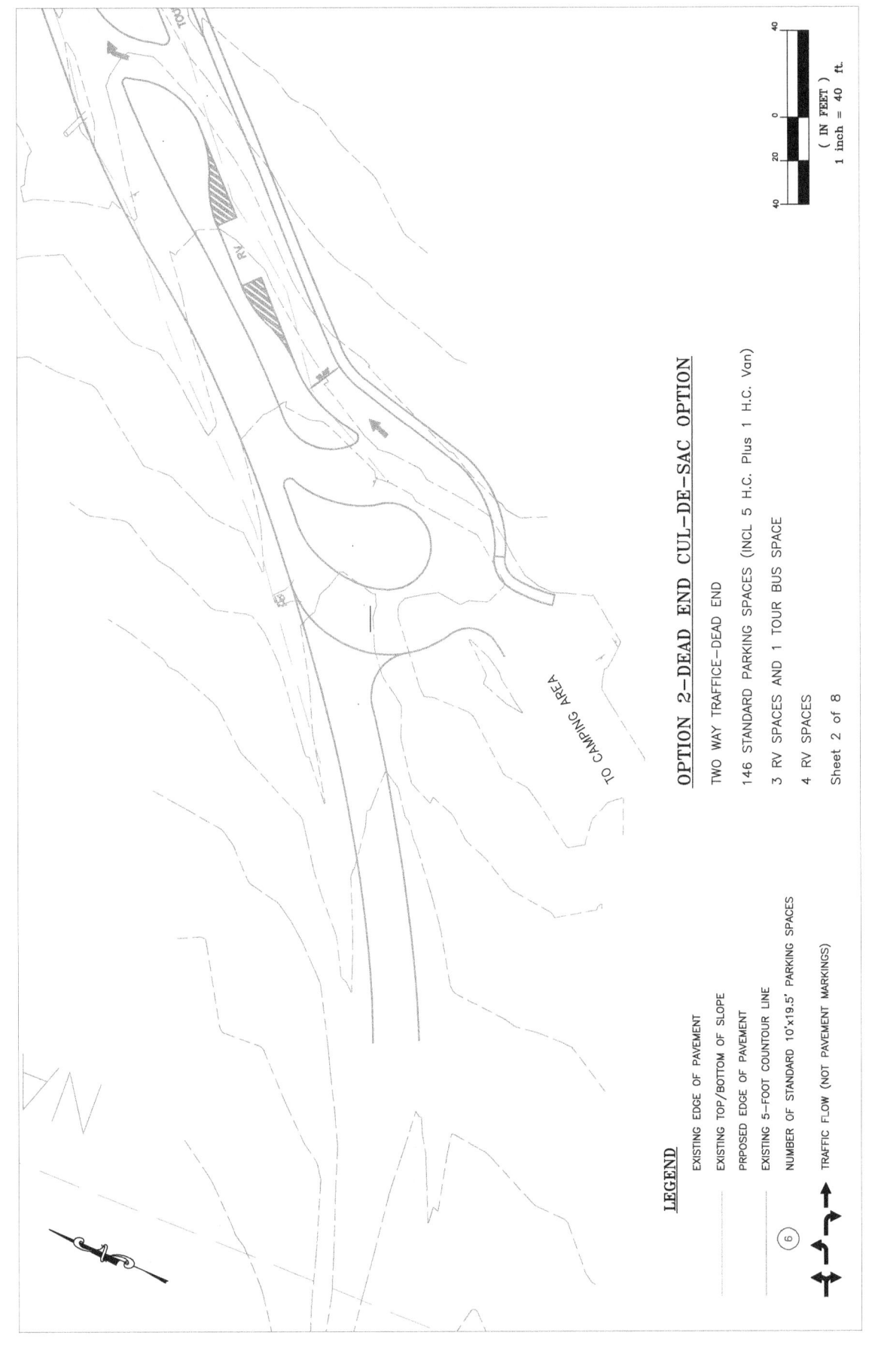

LEGEND

EXISTING EDGE OF PAVEMENT

EXISTING TOP/BOTTOM OF SLOPE

PRPOSED EDGE OF PAVEMENT

EXISTING 5-FOOT COUNTOUR LINE

NUMBER OF STANDARD 10'x19.5' PARKING SPACES

TRAFFIC FLOW (NOT PAVEMENT MARKINGS)

TO CAMPING AREA

OPTION 2–DEAD END CUL–DE–SAC OPTION

TWO WAY TRAFFICE–DEAD END

146 STANDARD PARKING SPACES (INCL 5 H.C. Plus 1 H.C. Van)

3 RV SPACES AND 1 TOUR BUS SPACE

4 RV SPACES

Sheet 2 of 8

(IN FEET)
1 inch = 40 ft.

RV

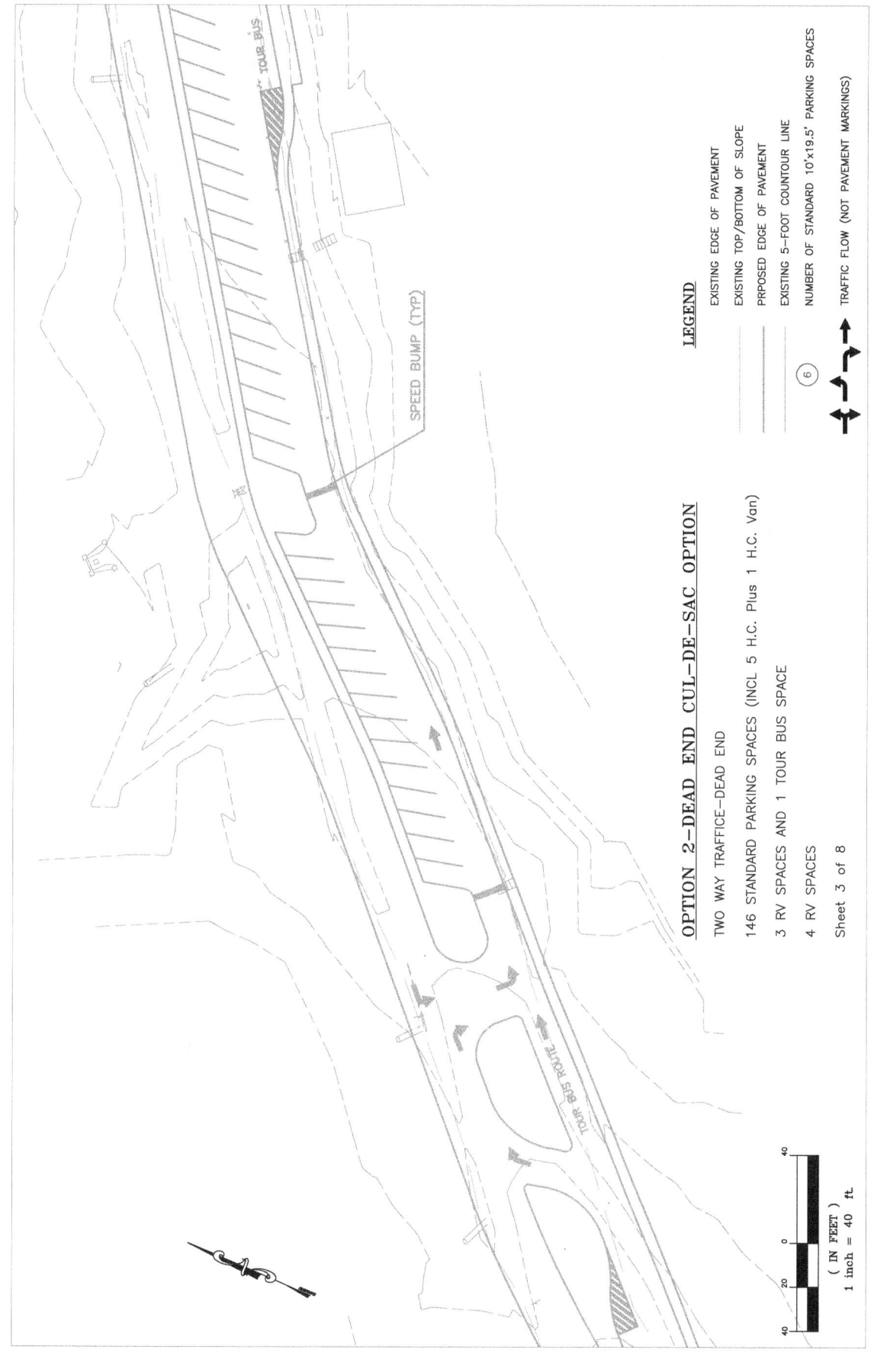

OPTION 2–DEAD END CUL–DE–SAC OPTION

TWO WAY TRAFFICE–DEAD END

146 STANDARD PARKING SPACES (INCL 5 H.C. Plus 1 H.C. Van)

3 RV SPACES AND 1 TOUR BUS SPACE

4 RV SPACES

Sheet 3 of 8

LEGEND

EXISTING EDGE OF PAVEMENT

EXISTING TOP/BOTTOM OF SLOPE

PRPOSED EDGE OF PAVEMENT

EXISTING 5–FOOT COUNTOUR LINE

NUMBER OF STANDARD 10'x19.5' PARKING SPACES

TRAFFIC FLOW (NOT PAVEMENT MARKINGS)

(IN FEET)
1 inch = 40 ft.

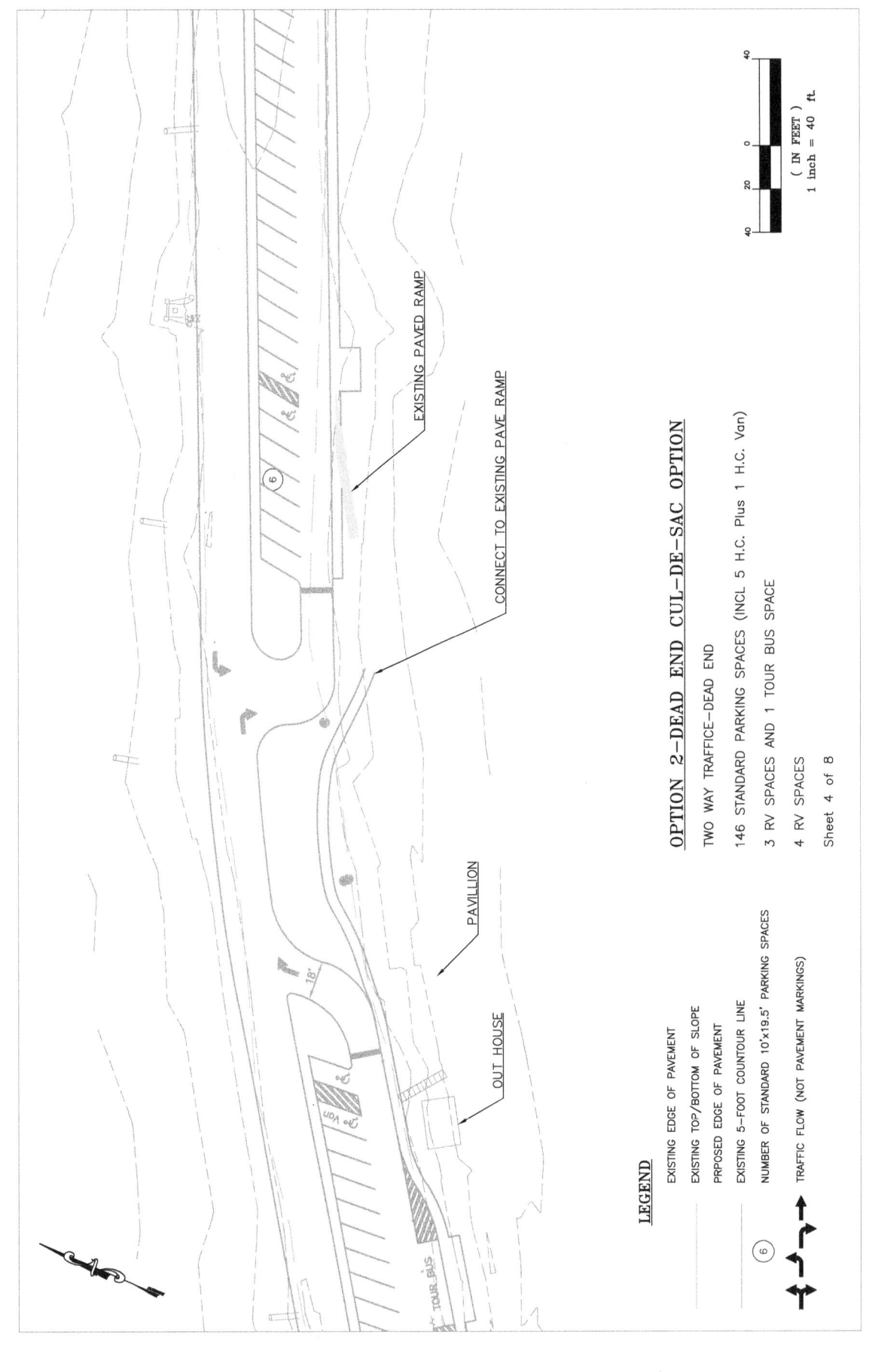

EXISTING PAVED RAMP

CONNECT TO EXISTING PAVE RAMP

6

PAVILLION

OUT HOUSE

18'

TOUR BUS

Van

LEGEND

EXISTING EDGE OF PAVEMENT

EXISTING TOP/BOTTOM OF SLOPE

PRPOSED EDGE OF PAVEMENT

EXISTING 5-FOOT COUNTOUR LINE

NUMBER OF STANDARD 10'x19.5' PARKING SPACES

TRAFFIC FLOW (NOT PAVEMENT MARKINGS)

6

OPTION 2-DEAD END CUL-DE-SAC OPTION

TWO WAY TRAFFICE—DEAD END

146 STANDARD PARKING SPACES (INCL 5 H.C. Plus 1 H.C. Van)

3 RV SPACES AND 1 TOUR BUS SPACE

4 RV SPACES

Sheet 4 of 8

(IN FEET)
1 inch = 40 ft.

40   20   0   40

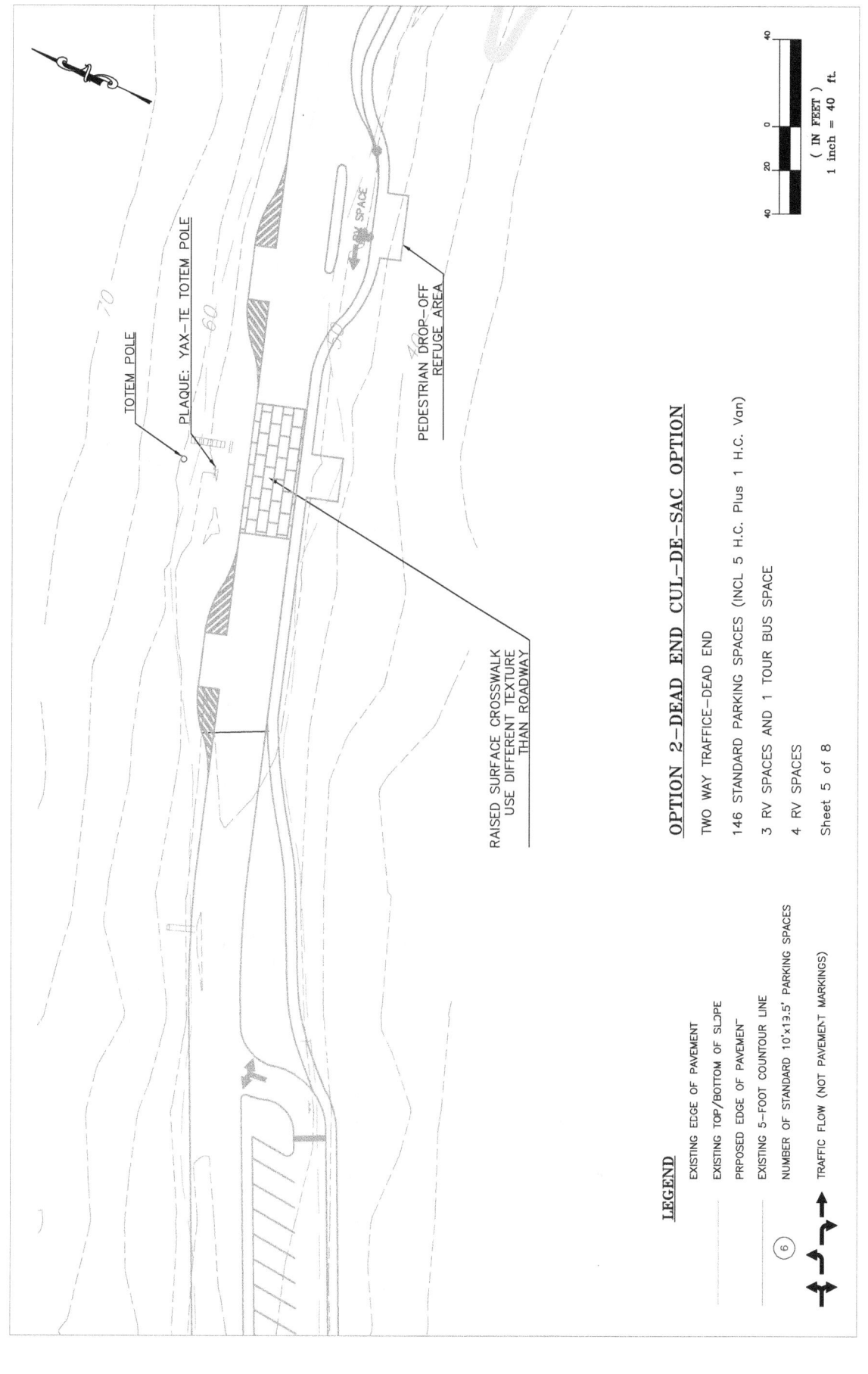

TOTEM POLE

PLAQUE: YAX-TE TOTEM POLE

RAISED SURFACE CROSSWALK
USE DIFFERENT TEXTURE
THAN ROADWAY

PEDESTRIAN DROP-OFF
REFUGE AREA

SPACE

OPTION 2-DEAD END CUL-DE-SAC OPTION

TWO WAY TRAFFICE-DEAD END

146 STANDARD PARKING SPACES (INCL 5 H.C. Plus 1 H.C. Van)

3 RV SPACES AND 1 TOUR BUS SPACE

4 RV SPACES

Sheet 5 of 8

LEGEND

EXISTING EDGE OF PAVEMENT

EXISTING TOP/BOTTOM OF SLOPE

PRPOSED EDGE OF PAVEMENT

EXISTING 5-FOOT COUNTOUR LINE

NUMBER OF STANDARD 10'x19.5' PARKING SPACES

TRAFFIC FLOW (NOT PAVEMENT MARKINGS)

(IN FEET)
1 inch = 40 ft.

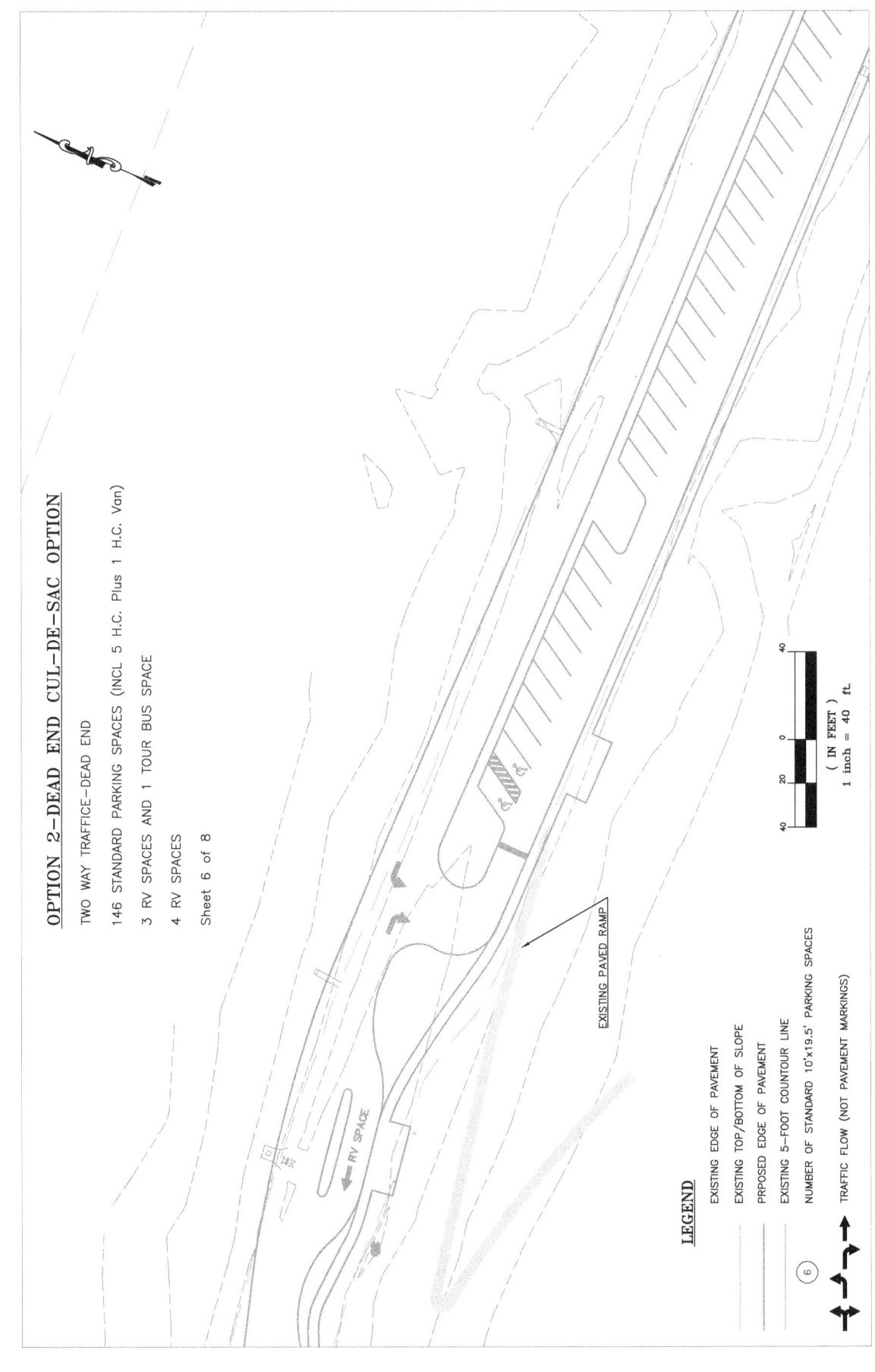

OPTION 2-DEAD END CUL-DE-SAC OPTION

TWO WAY TRAFFICE–DEAD END

146 STANDARD PARKING SPACES (INCL 5 H.C. Plus 1 H.C. Van)

3 RV SPACES AND 1 TOUR BUS SPACE

4 RV SPACES

Sheet 6 of 8

EXISTING PAVED RAMP

RV SPACE

LEGEND

EXISTING EDGE OF PAVEMENT

EXISTING TOP/BOTTOM OF SLOPE

PRPOSED EDGE OF PAVEMENT

EXISTING 5–FOOT COUNTOUR LINE

NUMBER OF STANDARD 10'x19.5' PARKING SPACES

TRAFFIC FLOW (NOT PAVEMENT MARKINGS)

(IN FEET)

1 inch = 40 ft.

40   20   0   40   40

6

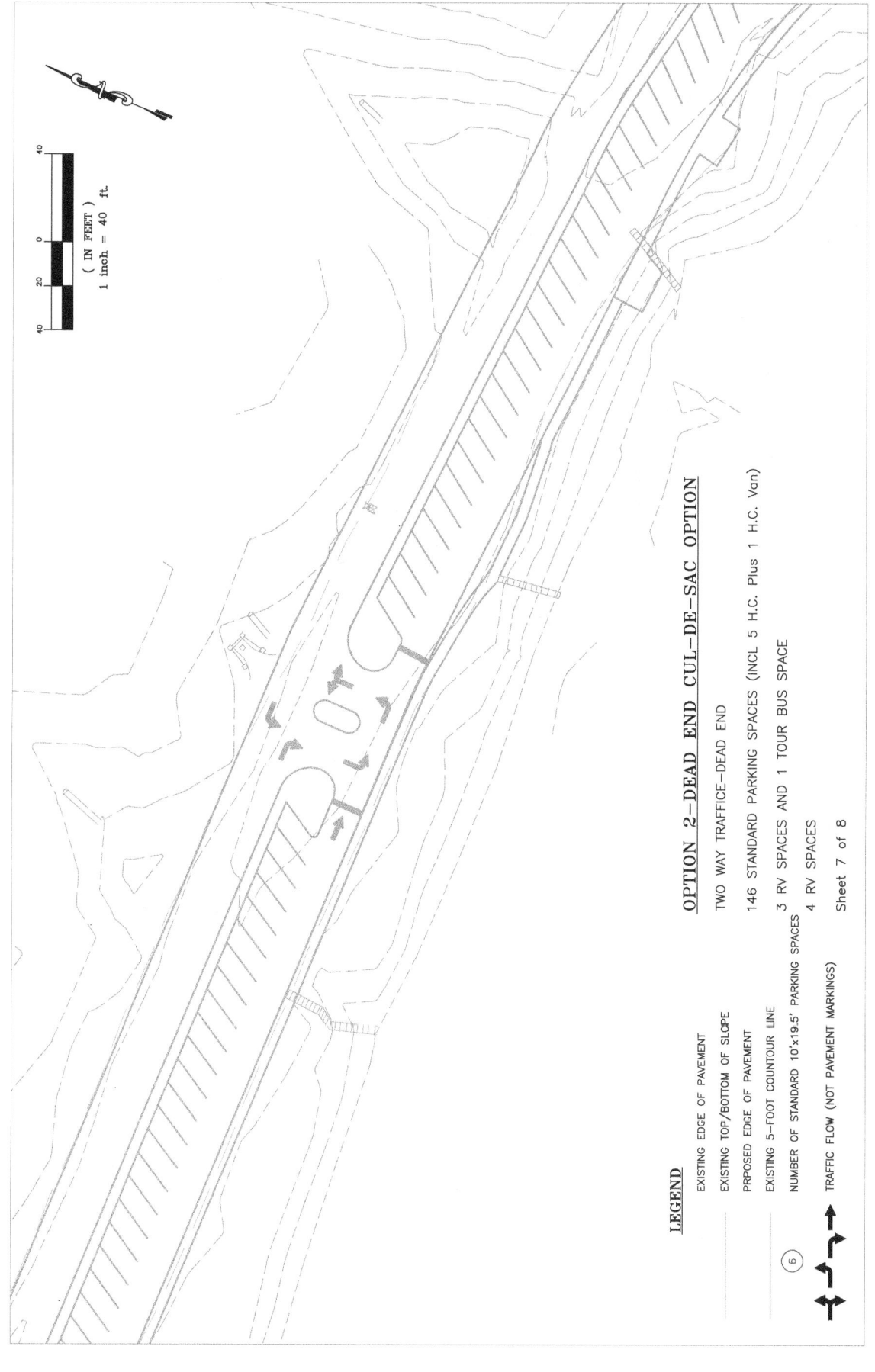

(IN FEET)
1 inch = 40 ft.

LEGEND

EXISTING EDGE OF PAVEMENT

EXISTING TOP/BOTTOM OF SLOPE

PRPOSED EDGE OF PAVEMENT

EXISTING 5-FOOT COUNTOUR LINE

NUMBER OF STANDARD 10'x19.5' PARKING SPACES

⑥

TRAFFIC FLOW (NOT PAVEMENT MARKINGS)

OPTION 2-DEAD END CUL-DE-SAC OPTION

TWO WAY TRAFFICE-DEAD END

146 STANDARD PARKING SPACES (INCL 5 H.C. Plus 1 H.C. Van)

3 RV SPACES AND 1 TOUR BUS SPACE

4 RV SPACES

Sheet 7 of 8

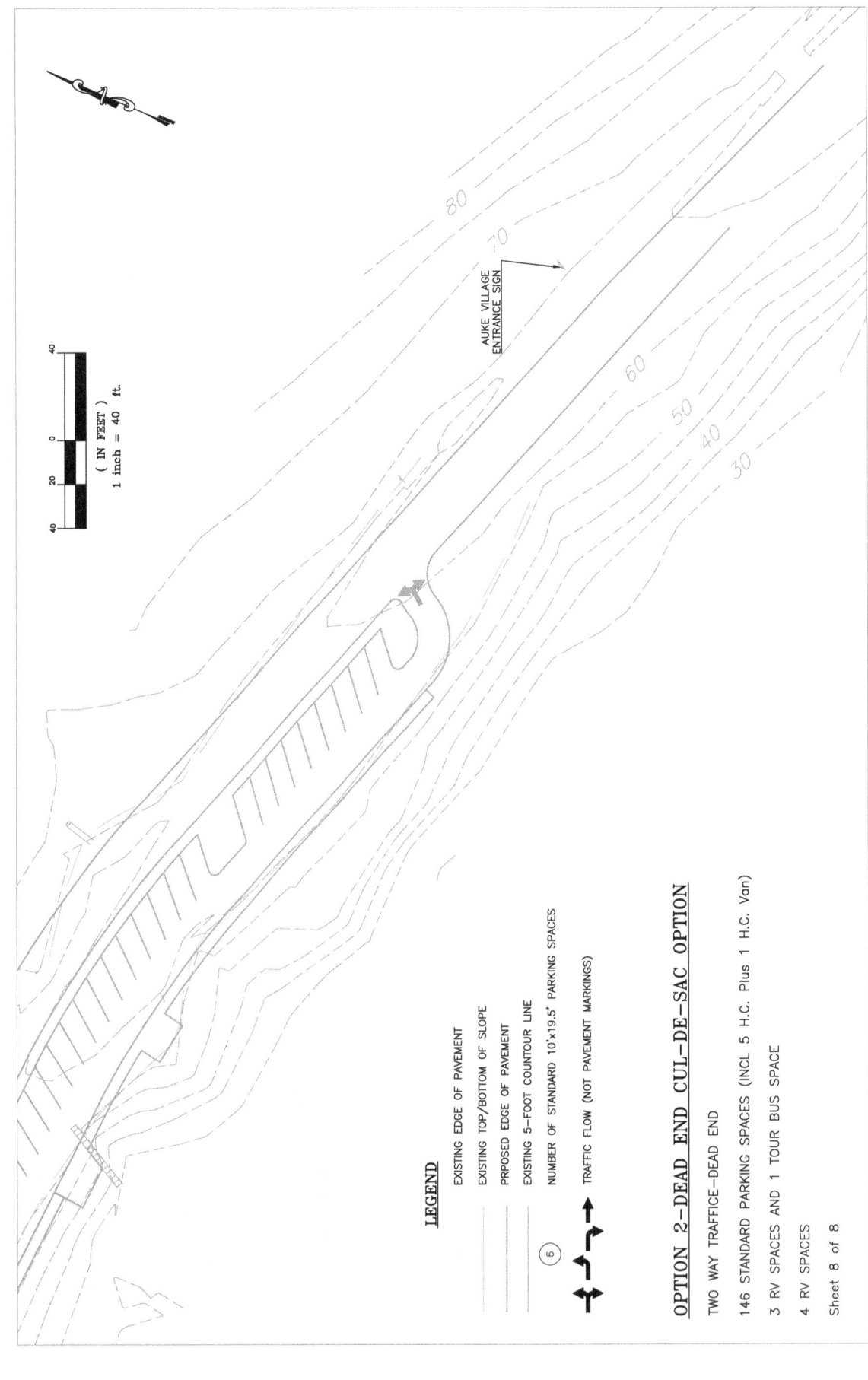

(IN FEET)
1 inch = 40 ft.

AUKE VILLAGE
ENTRANCE SIGN

80
70
60
50
40
30

<u>LEGEND</u>

EXISTING EDGE OF PAVEMENT

EXISTING TOP/BOTTOM OF SLOPE

PRPOSED EDGE OF PAVEMENT

EXISTING 5-FOOT COUNTOUR LINE

⑥ NUMBER OF STANDARD 10'x19.5' PARKING SPACES

TRAFFIC FLOW (NOT PAVEMENT MARKINGS)

OPTION 2-DEAD END CUL-DE-SAC OPTION

TWO WAY TRAFFICE-DEAD END

146 STANDARD PARKING SPACES (INCL 5 H.C. Plus 1 H.C. Van)

3 RV SPACES AND 1 TOUR BUS SPACE

4 RV SPACES

Sheet 8 of 8

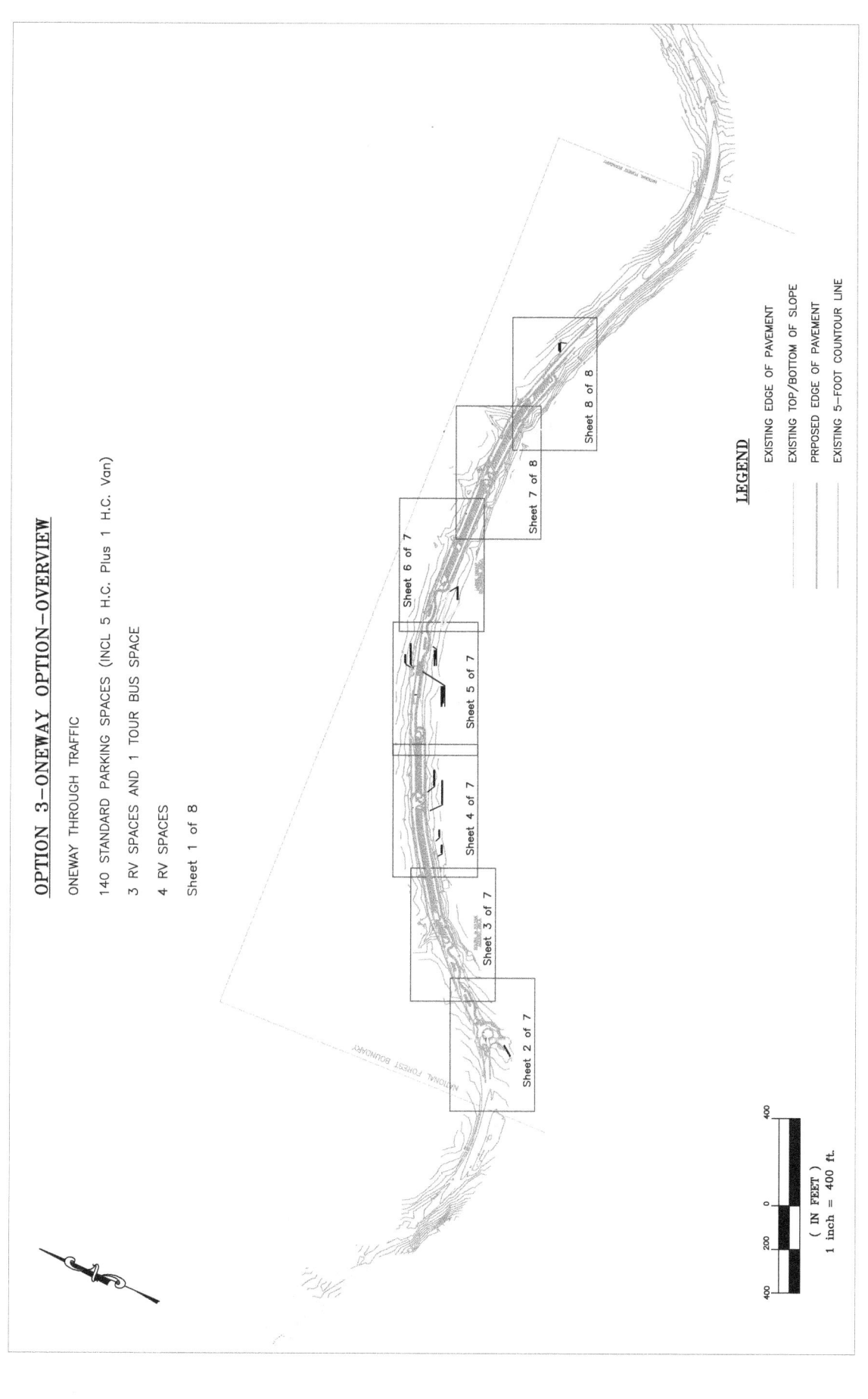

OPTION 3-ONEWAY OPTION-OVERVIEW

ONEWAY THROUGH TRAFFIC

140 STANDARD PARKING SPACES (INCL 5 H.C. Plus 1 H.C. Van)

3 RV SPACES AND 1 TOUR BUS SPACE

4 RV SPACES

Sheet 1 of 8

Sheet 2 of 7

Sheet 3 of 7

Sheet 4 of 7

Sheet 5 of 7

Sheet 6 of 7

Sheet 7 of 8

Sheet 8 of 8

NATIONAL FOREST BOUNDARY

LEGEND

EXISTING EDGE OF PAVEMENT

EXISTING TOP/BOTTOM OF SLOPE

PRPOSED EDGE OF PAVEMENT

EXISTING 5-FOOT COUNTOUR LINE

400   200   0   400

(IN FEET)
1 inch = 400 ft.

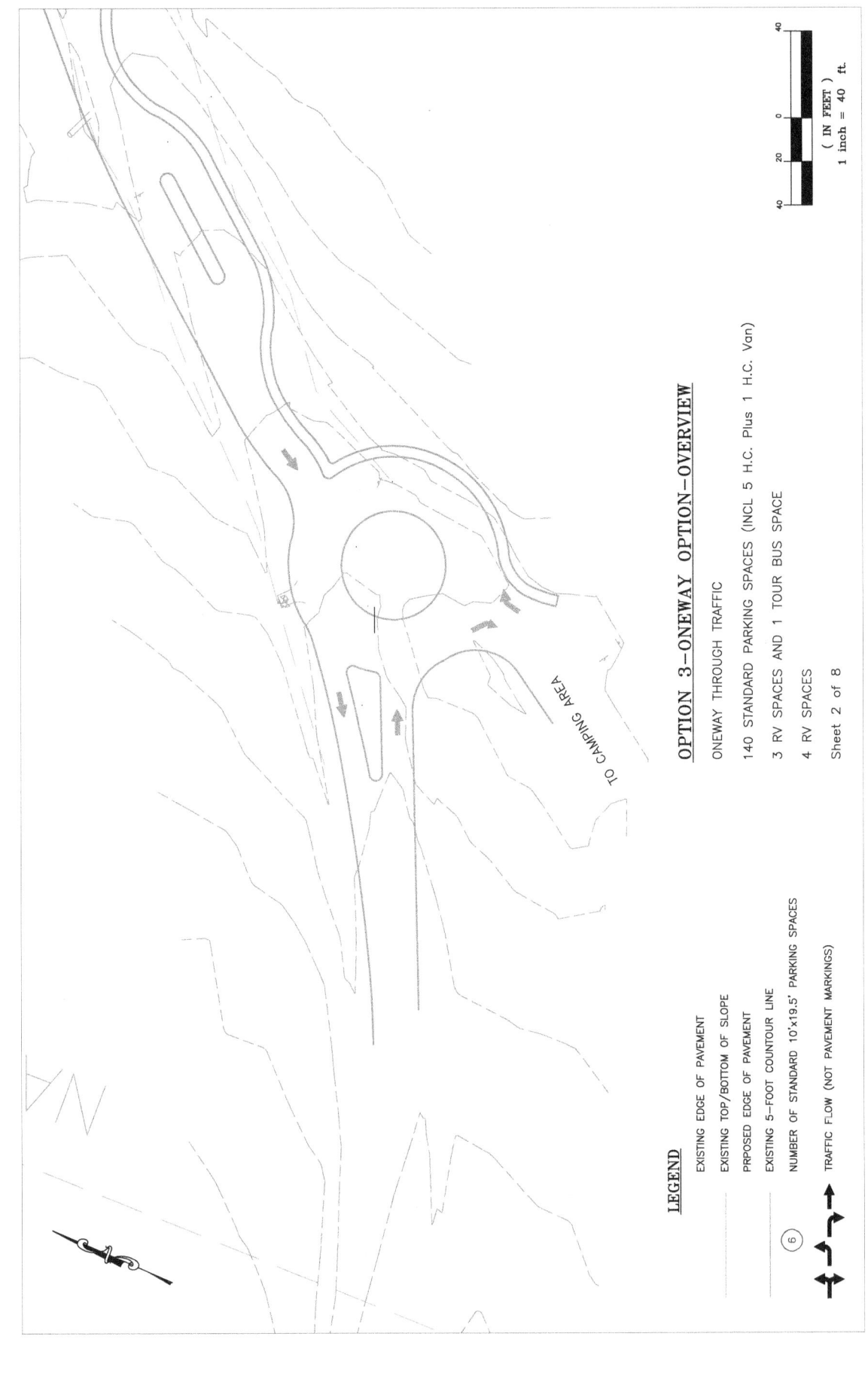

LEGEND

EXISTING EDGE OF PAVEMENT

EXISTING TOP/BOTTOM OF SLOPE

PRPOSED EDGE OF PAVEMENT

EXISTING 5-FOOT COUNTOUR LINE

NUMBER OF STANDARD 10'x19.5' PARKING SPACES

⑥

TRAFFIC FLOW (NOT PAVEMENT MARKINGS)

TO CAMPING AREA

OPTION 3-ONEWAY OPTION-OVERVIEW

ONEWAY THROUGH TRAFFIC

140 STANDARD PARKING SPACES (INCL 5 H.C. Plus 1 H.C. Van)

3 RV SPACES AND 1 TOUR BUS SPACE

4 RV SPACES

Sheet 2 of 8

(IN FEET)
1 inch = 40 ft.

40   20   0   40

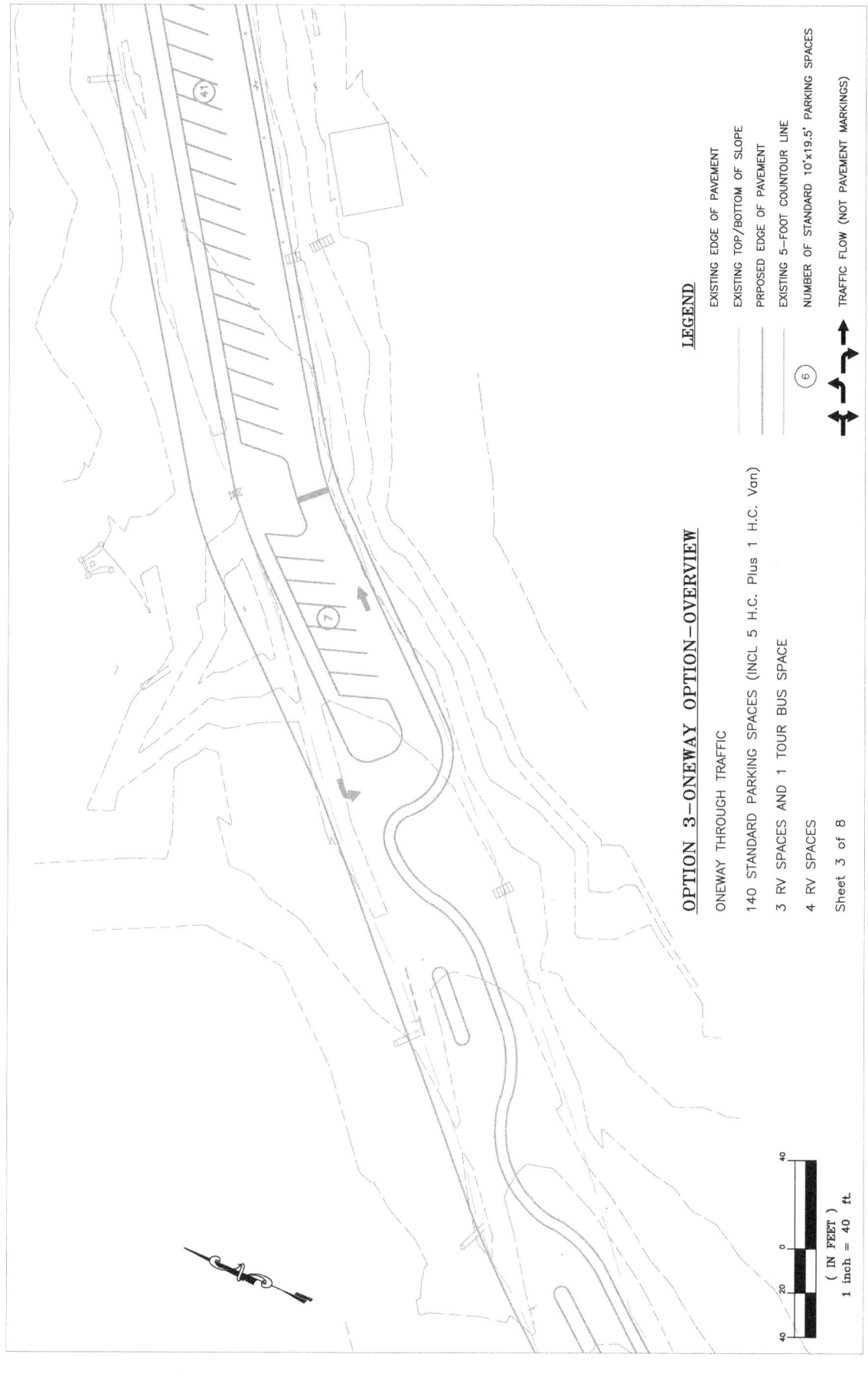

OPTION 3—ONEWAY OPTION—OVERVIEW

ONEWAY THROUGH TRAFFIC

140 STANDARD PARKING SPACES (INCL 5 H.C. Plus 1 H.C. Van)

3 RV SPACES AND 1 TOUR BUS SPACE

4 RV SPACES

Sheet 3 of 8

LEGEND

EXISTING EDGE OF PAVEMENT

EXISTING TOP/BOTTOM OF SLOPE

PRPOSED EDGE OF PAVEMENT

EXISTING 5-FOOT COUNTOUR LINE

NUMBER OF STANDARD 10'x19.5' PARKING SPACES

TRAFFIC FLOW (NOT PAVEMENT MARKINGS)

(IN FEET)
1 inch = 40 ft.

40   20   0   40

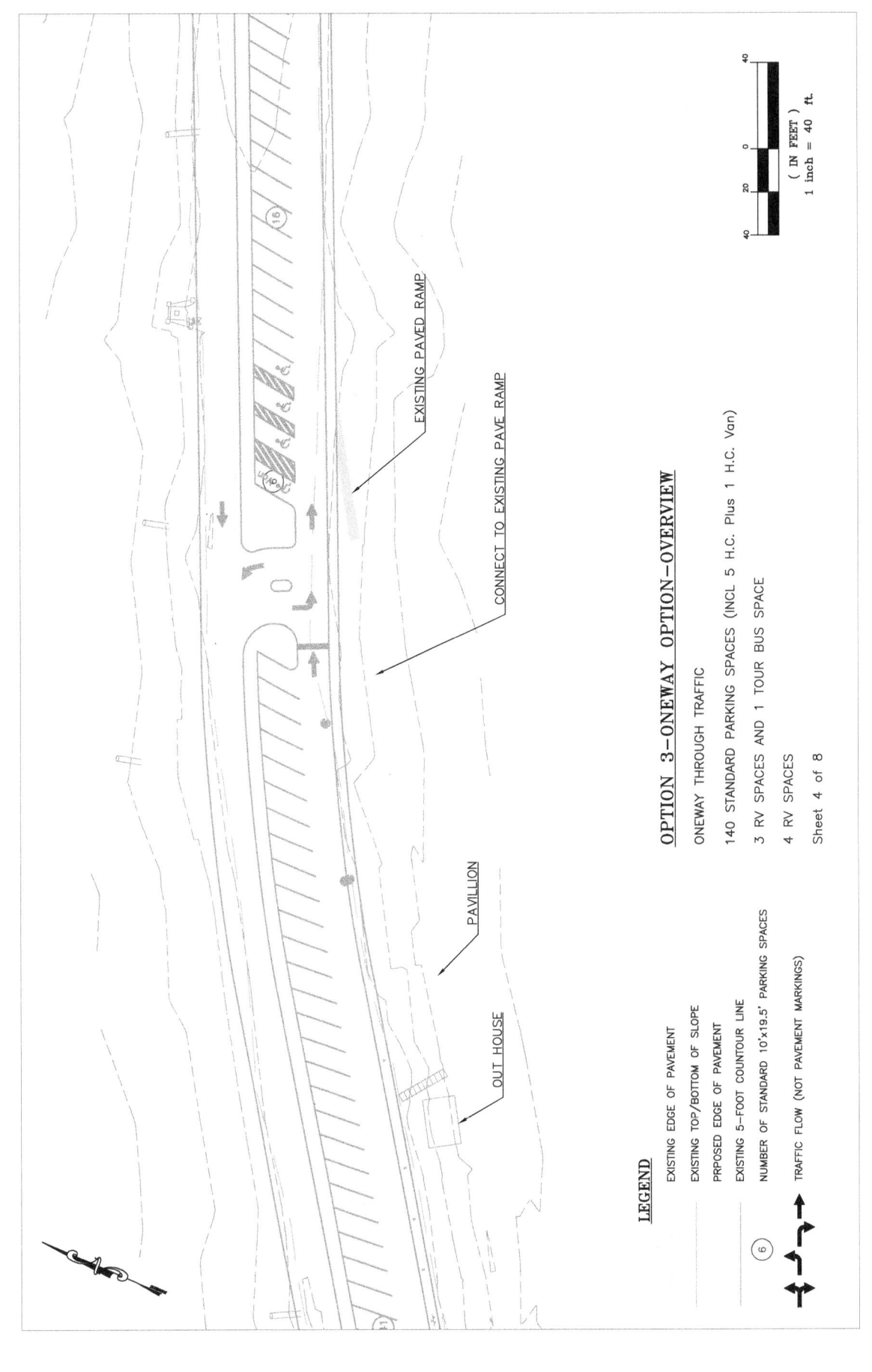

LEGEND

EXISTING EDGE OF PAVEMENT

EXISTING TOP/BOTTOM OF SLOPE

PRPOSED EDGE OF PAVEMENT

EXISTING 5-FOOT COUNTOUR LINE

NUMBER OF STANDARD 10'x19.5' PARKING SPACES

TRAFFIC FLOW (NOT PAVEMENT MARKINGS)

OUT HOUSE

PAVILLION

EXISTING PAVED RAMP

CONNECT TO EXISTING PAVE RAMP

OPTION 3-ONEWAY OPTION-OVERVIEW

ONEWAY THROUGH TRAFFIC

140 STANDARD PARKING SPACES (INCL 5 H.C. Plus 1 H.C. Van)

3 RV SPACES AND 1 TOUR BUS SPACE

4 RV SPACES

Sheet 4 of 8

(IN FEET)
1 inch = 40 ft.

40   20   0   40

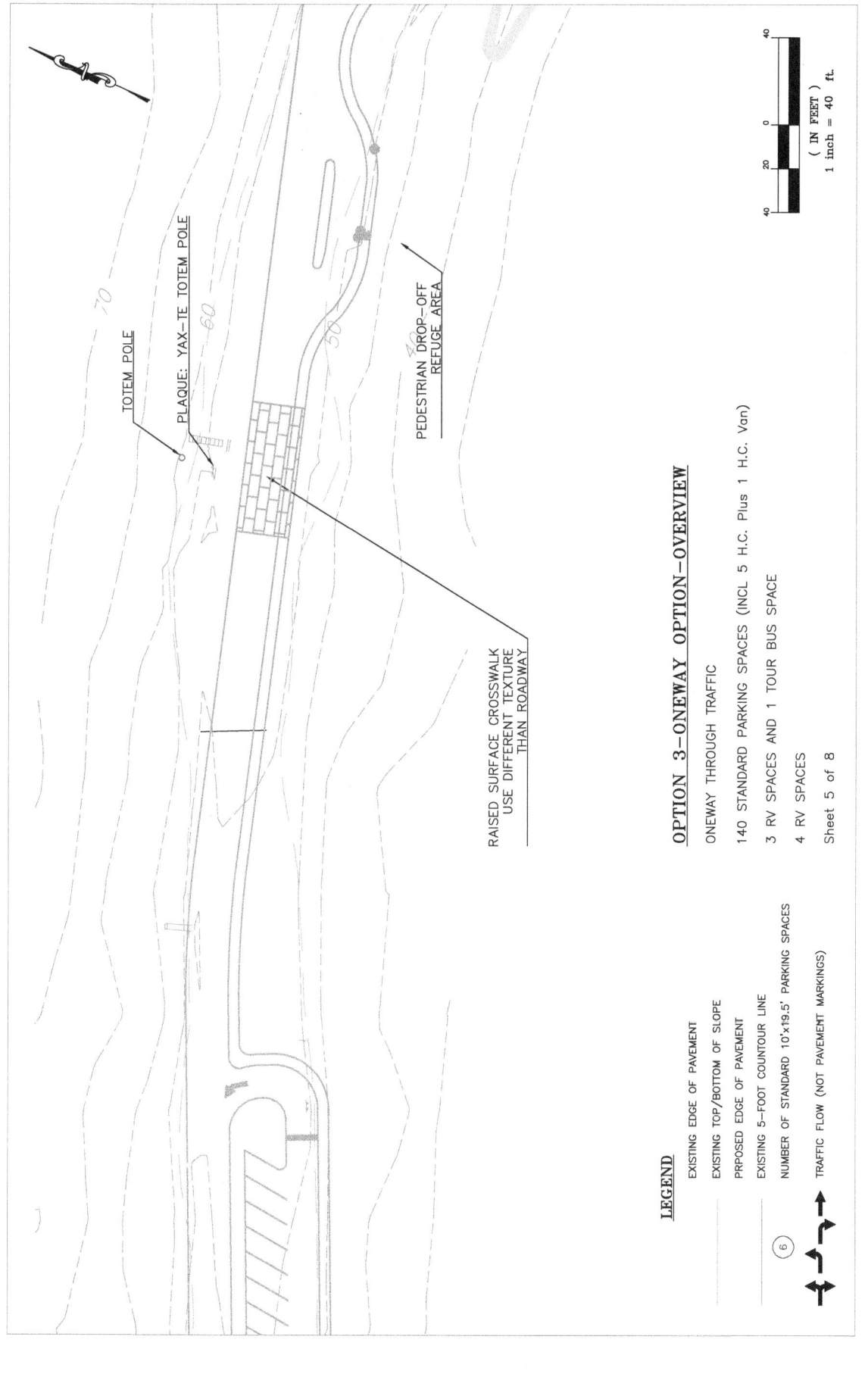

TOTEM POLE

PLAQUE: YAX-TE TOTEM POLE

RAISED SURFACE CROSSWALK
USE DIFFERENT TEXTURE
THAN ROADWAY

PEDESTRIAN DROP-OFF
REFUGE AREA

70

60

50

40

OPTION 3-ONEWAY OPTION-OVERVIEW

ONEWAY THROUGH TRAFFIC

140 STANDARD PARKING SPACES (INCL 5 H.C. Plus 1 H.C. Van)

3 RV SPACES AND 1 TOUR BUS SPACE

4 RV SPACES

Sheet 5 of 8

LEGEND

EXISTING EDGE OF PAVEMENT

EXISTING TOP/BOTTOM OF SLOPE

PRPOSED EDGE OF PAVEMENT

EXISTING 5-FOOT COUNTOUR LINE

NUMBER OF STANDARD 10'x19.5' PARKING SPACES

TRAFFIC FLOW (NOT PAVEMENT MARKINGS)

⑥

40   20   0   40

(IN FEET)
1 inch = 40 ft.

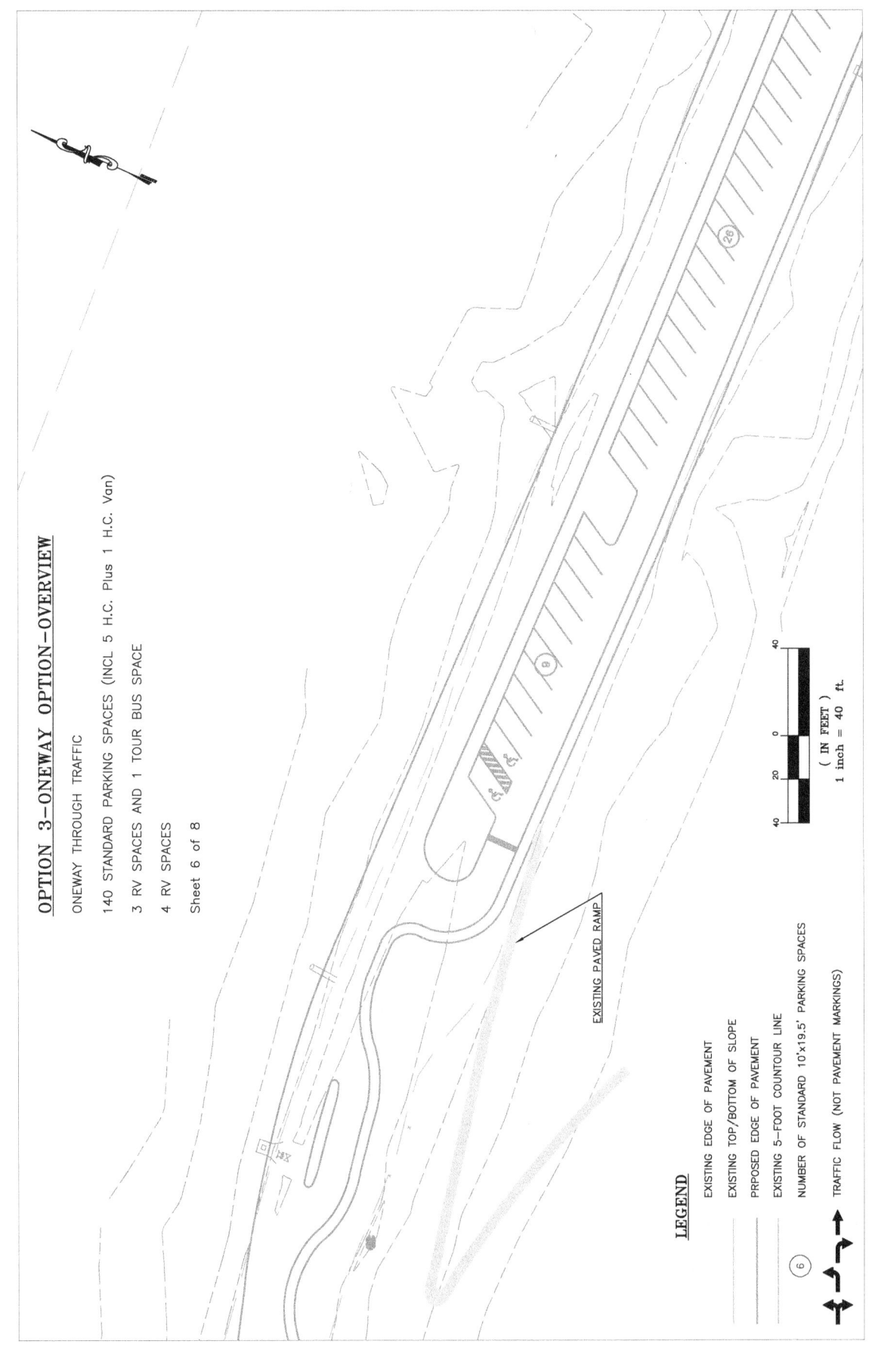

OPTION 3—ONEWAY OPTION—OVERVIEW

ONEWAY THROUGH TRAFFIC

140 STANDARD PARKING SPACES (INCL 5 H.C. Plus 1 H.C. Van)

3 RV SPACES AND 1 TOUR BUS SPACE

4 RV SPACES

Sheet 6 of 8

EXISTING PAVED RAMP

40   20   0   40

(IN FEET)
1 inch = 40   ft.

LEGEND

EXISTING EDGE OF PAVEMENT

EXISTING TOP/BOTTOM OF SLOPE

PRPOSED EDGE OF PAVEMENT

EXISTING 5-FOOT COUNTOUR LINE

NUMBER OF STANDARD 10'x19.5' PARKING SPACES

⑥

TRAFFIC FLOW (NOT PAVEMENT MARKINGS)

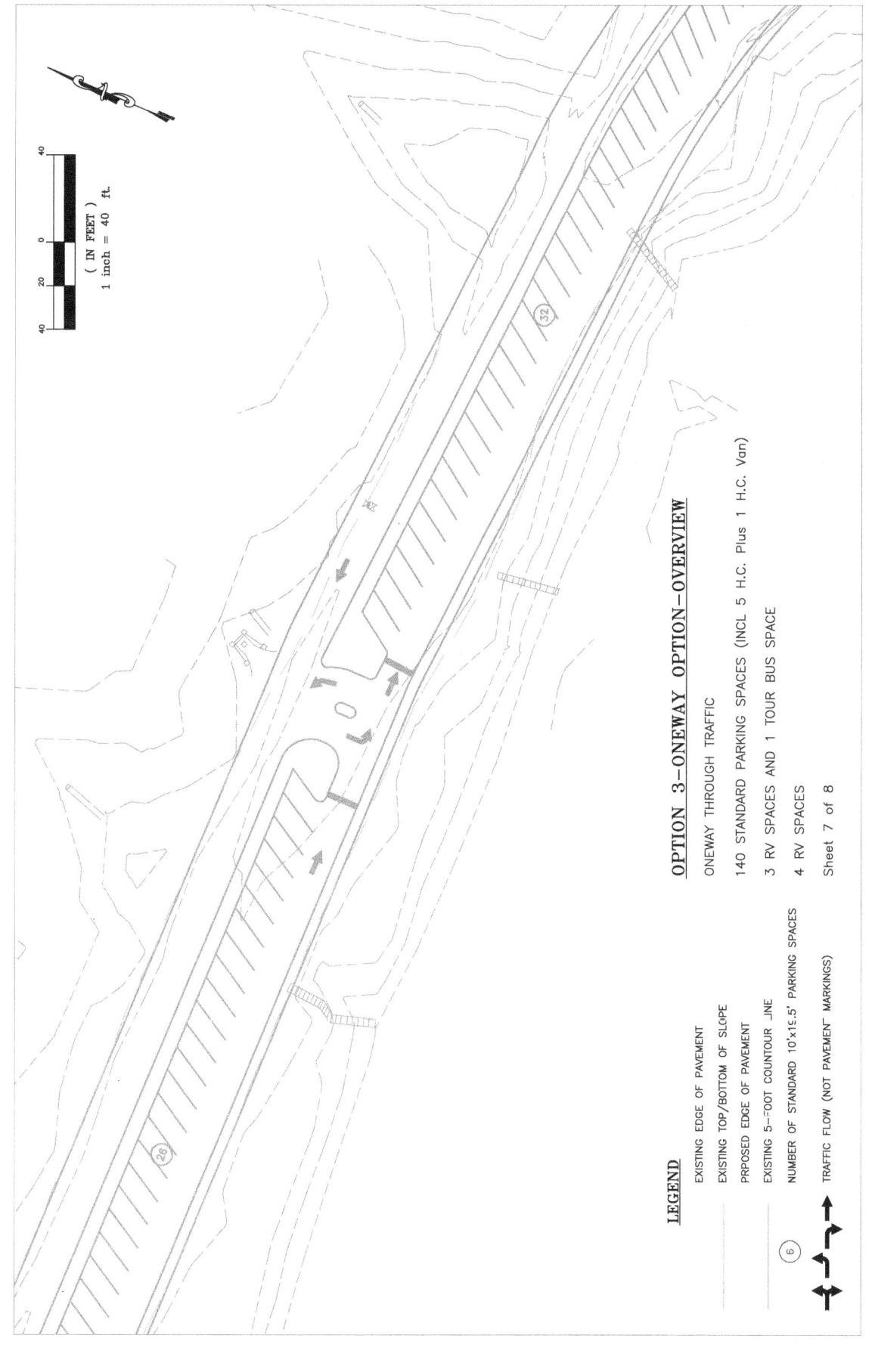

(IN FEET)
1 inch = 40 ft.

OPTION 3—ONEWAY OPTION—OVERVIEW

ONEWAY THROUGH TRAFFIC

140 STANDARD PARKING SPACES (INCL 5 H.C. Plus 1 H.C. Van)

3 RV SPACES AND 1 TOUR BUS SPACE

4 RV SPACES

Sheet 7 of 8

LEGEND

EXISTING EDGE OF PAVEMENT

EXISTING TOP/BOTTOM OF SLOPE

PRPOSED EDGE OF PAVEMENT

EXISTING 5-FOOT COUNTOUR LINE

NUMBER OF STANDARD 10'x15.5' PARKING SPACES

TRAFFIC FLOW (NOT PAVEMENT MARKINGS)

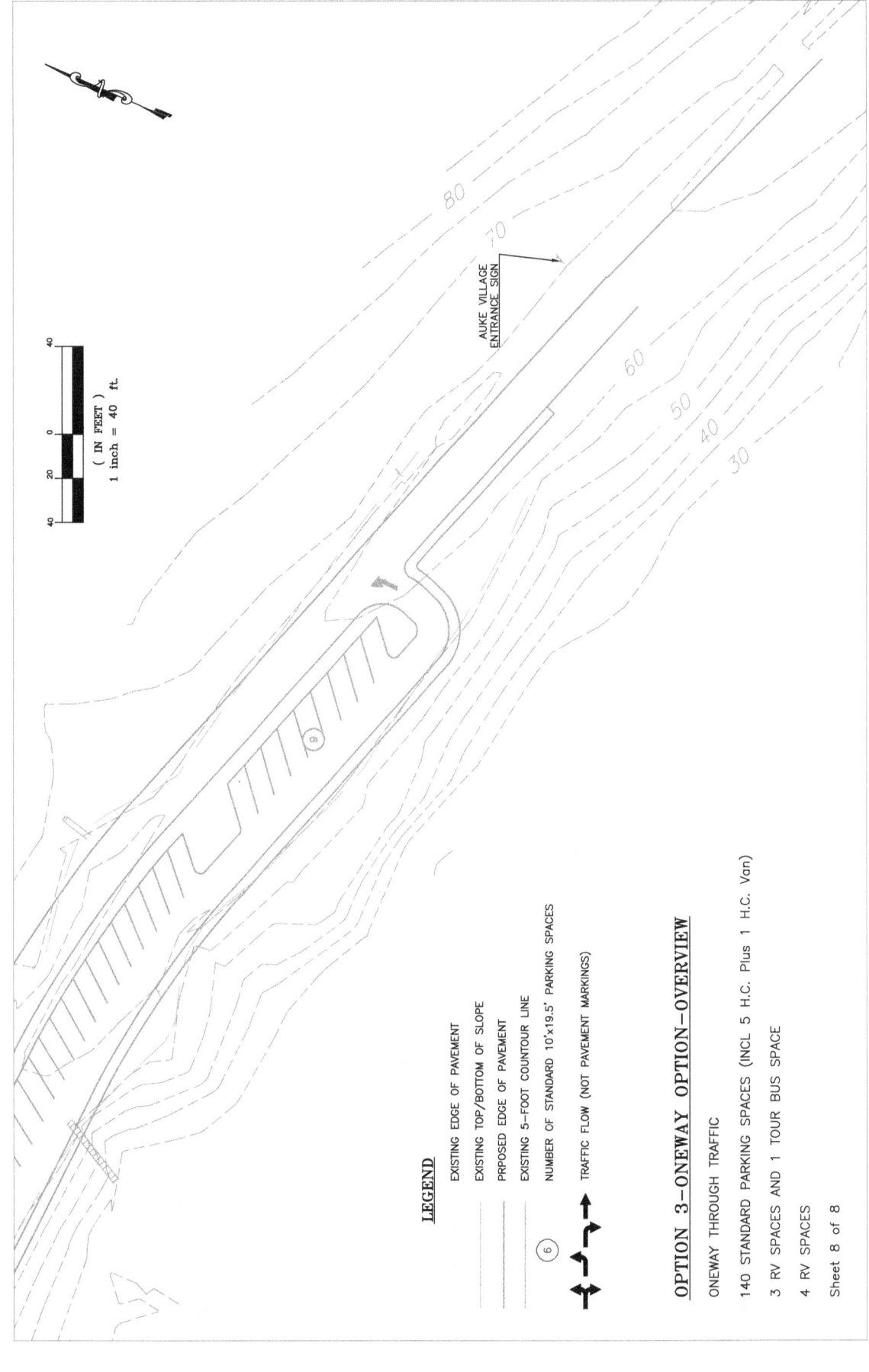

(IN FEET)
1 inch = 40 ft.

AUKE VILLAGE
ENTRANCE SIGN

LEGEND

EXISTING EDGE OF PAVEMENT

EXISTING TOP/BOTTOM OF SLOPE

PRPOSED EDGE OF PAVEMENT

EXISTING 5-FOOT COUNTOUR LINE

NUMBER OF STANDARD 10'x19.5' PARKING SPACES

TRAFFIC FLOW (NOT PAVEMENT MARKINGS)

OPTION 3-ONEWAY OPTION-OVERVIEW

ONEWAY THROUGH TRAFFIC

140 STANDARD PARKING SPACES (INCL 5 H.C. Plus 1 H.C. Van)

3 RV SPACES AND 1 TOUR BUS SPACE

4 RV SPACES

Sheet 8 of 8